Dating
the second
time around
Finding love that lasts

eHarmony®

hamlyn

The relationship advice in this book applies to any type of romantic relationship. The terms "he" or "she" or "Mr. and Mrs." are used interchangeably throughout the text.

An Hachette UK Company
www.hachette.co.uk

First published in Great Britain in 2010 by Hamlyn a division of Octopus Publishing Group Ltd, Endeavour House, 189 Shaftesbury Avenue, London, WC2H 8JY
www.octopusbooks.co.uk

Distributed in the USA and Canada by Octopus Books USA: c/o Hachette Book Group USA, 237 Park Avenue, New York, NY 10017, USA
www.octopusbooksusa.com

ISBN-13: 978-0-600-62227-7

A CIP catalogue record for this book is available from the British Library.

Printed and bound in the UK

10 9 8 7 6 5 4 3 2 1

Dating

the second time around

Finding love that lasts

General editor
Dr Gian Gonzaga Ph.D
eHarmony®

hamlyn

Contents

Foreword

Relationships are hard. They don't start off feeling hard; in fact, most of the time they feel easy at first. Everything seems to flow. You want to spend all of your time together. You have lots to talk about, and a seemingly endless supply of new activities to try. But eventually all relationships go through hard times when you don't have as much to talk about, or the stress of life means you argue a lot more, or your kids are keeping you from getting enough sleep so you are both grumpy. These hard times are when you learn about the true quality of the relationship. Can you depend on your partner to be there to support you, even if they are not feeling well themselves? Will your partner take the time to understand your point of view, even when you are fighting? Would you sacrifice your own career so your partner could get the job of their dreams?

This book isn't about preparing you for the easy times. It isn't about the giddy high of the honeymoon period when you are getting along well. This book is about how to find a partner who will be there with you during the hard times. That's what makes a great relationship. When you find someone with whom you can make it through the tough times, the good times become all the sweeter.

This kind of advice may resonate, particularly when you are coming back to dating a second time. If you are divorced you will be well aware of how a relationship can go wrong, and how problems, stress, and basic incompatibility can lead to the demise of an otherwise strong partnership. You may be a bit hesitant going into a new relationship, because you feel as though you just got burned, or you are worried about making the same mistakes again. Perhaps it's been so long that you barely remember how to date, or where to find someone new.

Well, take heart. Your past experiences can help you to have a better relationship the next time around. You don't have to be doomed to repeat the same mistakes again. You have a better idea of the characteristics and values that are most important to you, and the ones you need to have in a partner. You have experience in a long-term relationship and as long as you learn from that experience you can make your next relationship stronger and better.

This is written by the experts at eHarmony, one of the world's leading relationship websites. I am the head of the company's Research and Development department. Over the years eHarmony has studied thousands and thousands of couples in dozens of countries to uncover what people should look for in a partner before they start a relationship. eHarmony has a dedicated relationship advice team and half-a-dozen researchers with Ph.Ds in psychology, who have been studying relationships for a combined total of over sixty years. We collaborate with some of the finest researchers in the world to uncover what makes a relationship work—not for a day, or a month, or a year, but for a lifetime.

Our work is based on research and science. Our advice is based on studies of singles who are still looking for relationships, dating couples in the throes of passionate love, and couples who have been married for many years. The advice we give is based on the distilled wisdom of thousands of people who between them have been in relationships for many years. Some of our findings come from work we have done at eHarmony, and some of them are from researchers who have spent decades studying relationships at the world's finest universities. So this book isn't just advice that one person has gleaned from their own experience, or the experiences of their friends; it comes from the combined experiences of many thousands of people worldwide.

The first section of the book helps you learn lessons about yourself (chapter one), what could have gone wrong the last time (chapter two), how you can find someone who is compatible (chapter three), and what you want in a partner (chapter four). These are critical lessons to take on board before searching for a partner. These chapters will help you learn from your past and apply this wisdom to finding a new partner in a way that will help you avoid the mistakes you made before and discover what are the genuinely important qualities in a partner. Everyone should go through this kind of analysis before they start a relationship. Coming back a second time, you will have special insight into these questions.

The second section of the book helps you in the early stages of dating and starting a new relationship: how to find a partner (chapter five), the first date (chapter six), the early weeks (chapter seven), and making a new relationship work (chapter eight). These are lessons you may have forgotten since the last time you dated and might need a refresher on. Guess what? Many of these things haven't changed. People still get nervous on first dates, and the first weeks of a relationship can still be enthralling. But other things have changed. You may not want to hang out in bars any more, college is a long time ago, and most of your friends may be married. Don't worry, though. With the rise of Internet dating, it is much easier to find people in the same position as you: looking for a relationship and wondering where to find one. Now there is a place.

The final section of the book looks forward to a time when your relationship has become established. What are the special challenges for second-timers in relationships (chapter nine), how can you prepare for commitment (chapter ten), and how can you keep things fresh and fun (chapter eleven)? These are issues you can think about and plan for now. The more you prepare for the future, the better that future will be.

Relationships are worth having. A good relationship can make you happier, a better parent, more successful in your job, and can make you live longer. But a bad relationship can drag you down, lead to depression, fights, and illness. With all you have learned, you now have the power to take control of your next relationship and make sure it is better, stronger, and more satisfying than your last one. Good luck and have fun.

Gian Gonzaga, Ph.D

CHAPTER ONE

Looking at You

In the 21st century, few of us marry our high school or college sweethearts and stay with them till death do us part. Life is more complicated than it used to be and offers us many more choices. On the whole, this is wonderful. We have more career, economic, social, and sexual freedom than our parents and grandparents had. Not many people would want to turn back the clock.

One side effect of this freedom is that we are now able to move on from less-than-satisfactory relationships, rather than being trapped for decades with Mr. or Mrs. Totally Wrong. How many of us know elderly couples living in the same house who obviously can't stand each other? For religious, financial, or social reasons, they stay together, picking away at each other like woodpeckers, both too set in their ways to try and change.

You're lucky. You don't have to do this. You have choices when you're ready to exercise them.

It can be daunting to look for another relationship when you've been committed to someone for years. The world of dating has changed, and there will be times when you may feel left behind or out of sync. There may be days when you think you'll never find someone new. But don't despair, and don't give up. Believe it or not, you are in a position of strength. You have been through a relationship before, and, even if it ended bitterly, you learned lessons that can help you grow personally and find another, better relationship.

If you approach the search in the right spirit and are willing to try new things, you can make wiser choices than when you were in your teens or early twenties. Here's why:

- You know yourself better. You know what you want, what you believe in, and who you are. This makes it easier to look for someone with the same outlook.
- You developed relationship skills the last time around. You have likely had to resolve conflict, share your space, and make major life decisions about issues such as buying a home or having children. These experiences can help you adapt better to a new relationship.
- You can learn from any mistakes you've made. Maybe you chose the wrong partner, let work stress sour your relationship, or didn't handle conflicts well. Whatever those mistakes were, they offer valuable lessons you can use in your next relationship.

The journey to find love again may not be easy. You may have to confront some uncomfortable truths about yourself. Social norms and new technologies have changed the way people meet and date, so you will have to adapt. And when you do find someone, you will have to adjust to their personal habits and quirks.

But all this is worth it. Good relationships can make you happier, more successful, and can even make you live longer. With all of your experience, and with a little help from the advice in this book, you have a great chance of finding lasting love.

The first step in finding a new relationship is to take an honest view of yourself, and the qualities you have to bring to a partnership. We'll go through this process in chapter one. The second step is to assess what happened in your last relationship. We'll look at this in detail in chapter two.

All relationships, no matter how long they lasted, how much pain they caused, or how poorly they ended, worked in some ways and didn't work in other ways. Analyzing what worked, and what didn't work; which problems arose that you and your partner successfully negotiated, and which tripped you up; the things you did that made the relationship more satisfying and those that made it more difficult, will help you to decide what qualities to look for in your next partner. This is addressed in chapters three and four.

And then we'll go on to discuss where you can meet this new person and how to handle the relationship in the early stages.

But first of all, let's find out—who are *you*?

YOUR UNIQUE QUALITIES

Throughout this book you will find written exercises to help you focus your thoughts. It's worth buying a notebook in which to write your answers, so they are all kept in the same place. Your dating notebook will track your journey toward a new relationship and highlight milestones you pass along the way.

For the first exercise, on page one of your notebook list five great qualities that you have to offer in a relationship and five not-so-great qualities about yourself that make your relationships more difficult. These could be practical skills, such as being a great cook—or lousy cleaner; emotional ones, such as being loyal and supportive—or jealous and mistrusting; or social ones, such as being good at making others laugh—or not being able to remember people's names.

When you have finished your list, show it to your best friend, a family member, or someone else you trust to see if they agree with your choices. Often, how we see ourselves is not the same way as others see us. Their perceptions will help you get a clearer picture of who you are and the way you come across to others.

Your self-concept

Think back to your fifteen-year-old self. Get out some old photographs if you can bear it. What kind of music did you like then? Did you have one of the era's high-fashion hairstyles that looked as though you had stuck your fingers in a plug socket? What was your taste in clothes—or is it too embarrassing even to contemplate?

Think about the values and beliefs you held at that age. Were you politically conscious, or religiously motivated? Did you think that career or family was more important?

How much have your beliefs changed since then?

There have been hundreds of research studies over the years analyzing what makes good relationships work. Scientists have looked at couples that have been together for ten, twenty, thirty years, or more. They've identified many things that predict whether people remain happy or satisfied with their relationship after all that time. You probably won't be surprised to hear that conflict resolution skills are important. Having great sex every night isn't. Getting along with the in-laws helps. Whether or not you have children together is immaterial. Through all this scientific research, one consistent predictor of relationship satisfaction has emerged: whether the individuals have certain core characteristics, values, and beliefs in common.

> *Having core traits and values in common is a powerful predictor of whether a relationship will work long term.*

At the age of fifteen, only a very savvy few of us knew what we wanted to do with our lives and who we wanted to be. During adolescence and young adulthood, we are still coming to understand our own personalities and to shape our sense of identity. Most of us experiment with different self-concepts, just as we try different "looks" and evolve, say, from preppie to goth to business suits. We keep evolving through our teens and twenties. As we find the elements that we feel most comfortable with, or our social circumstances begin to constrain us, our sense of identity solidifies and is less changeable over time.

Those who get into a long-term relationship in their teens may find they are able to grow in the same direction as their partner, but there's an element of luck involved. Now that you are older, you will have a clearer concept of yourself and your values and so will your potential partners. This means you can select someone whose worldview matches yours in all the important respects. You've tried more things and figured out what is going to be critical for you. With a little self-reflection to understand what qualities are the most important, you will be better placed to make good choices from the outset.

This doesn't mean you should be stuck in your ways. Being open to change is crucial if you are going to invite someone to share your life. In fact, making any necessary changes before you start searching for Mr. or Mrs. Right will help you present your best self to potential partners. They will see what a great individual you are, and you will come out of it a better person than when you started.

GROWTH ORIENTATION
To find a relationship and make it work, you need to take control over the process by searching for the right type of partner, and acting to ensure the quality of the resulting relationship. Amazingly, lots of people sit at home expecting Prince or Princess Charming magically to arrive at the front door and whisk them off their feet. They think that whether it works out or not will be down to fate or the cosmos or astrological compatibility rather than anything they might do or not do.

Those who believe that finding (or keeping) a great relationship is a matter of luck or destiny are in for disappointment. Those who believe they can control whether a relationship works or not will ultimately be happier. Psychologists call this "locus of control."

Some people have an external locus of control, which means they don't think they have the power to change things. Others have an internal locus of control, which means that they believe they can change their situation with some effort. Those who have an internal locus of control more often try to make things better rather than passively accepting their fate, and that alone makes a big difference.

Contrast the following statements:

"If I am meant for a great relationship it will find me."
versus
"I can do things that make it more likely I will find a great relationship."

"If my relationship fails, it is because it wasn't meant to be."
versus
"All relationships can be made better by working at them."

"Finding a great relationship is the luck of the draw."
versus
"Great relationships take time and effort."

Which approach do you think is likeliest to be more successful?
Which approach have you tended to take so far?
Is it time for you to think about changing your locus of control?

Before you start dating...

There are many ways to start taking control of your life. Before you start searching for a new partner, you might feel that you want to lose weight, stop smoking, or make other personal changes so that you attract a particular type of person. But that means you are doing it for external reasons; you are doing it *for them*. Giving up bad habits for the sake of someone else will never work over the long term. You'll only stick to a new regime if you do it for internal reasons, in order to take better care of yourself. It's all about having a healthy sense of self-worth.

However, taking care of yourself can in turn help you create a successful new relationship. Part of the reason for this is obvious: you may end up being a better partner. The healthier your diet, and the better the quality of sleep you get, the more able you will be to deal with stressful situations—and as we all know, relationships can be extremely stressful. When you're out of shape and sleep-deprived, you are apt to make poorer decisions, fail at tasks, not cope well with stress. This can lead to having nastier arguments with your partner because your mental and physical resources to deal with stress are not as sharp as they could be.

Imagine that your partner comes home from work after a miserable day and really needs to be able to vent to you. If you are exhausted and stressed, you're less likely to have the emotional energy to listen and be empathetic.

There is another benefit to taking care of yourself for your own benefit: it will give you an internal locus of control. You will come to believe that you can change things if you need to. This feeds into other areas of life. If you are in debt, you will be more likely to get debt counseling and advice to come up with a repayment plan. If you don't like your job, you will be more likely to start looking for a new one. If you want to start a great relationship, you will take control of searching for the right partner.

This may not be as easy if you have had an external locus of control for most of your life. You might not even see a way to take control. If the problems seem insurmountable, you should consider consulting a therapist or a life coach. There's always a way through. At first you may need help seeing that, but sooner or later it will come more naturally to you.

> *Change what you can to make yourself healthier and happier, but do it for yourself, rather than some potential partner you haven't yet met.*

Don't keep putting off your search for Mr. or Mrs. Right just because you are in debt or are a bit overweight. Self-improvement is an ongoing personal journey. If you keep making excuses not to start dating again, you won't. You have to start by taking the first step and putting yourself out there.

P. J. and Tina

P. J. had been divorced for about three years. He dated several women before becoming thoroughly fed up with the bar scene and unsatisfactory blind dates. He knew exactly what he wanted in a partner and a relationship, so he joined an online relationship site where he thought he could find someone who shared those qualities. Tina was the first person he met through the site. Soon after meeting, each realized that the other person was exactly whom they had been looking for—it was almost uncanny. In Tina, P. J. found his best friend, lover, his everything—just as she did with him. They were married in 2007 and are still crazy about each other.

Be your most attractive self

Our culture tends to equate attractiveness first and foremost with physical appearance. These expectations can be unrealistic, frustrating, and demoralizing, sending us negative messages about ourselves. In the end, your physical appearance is part of your total attractiveness package, but your manner, your outlook, and the way you engage with people can be as important as what you look like.

By all means, get a makeover if you want. Ask your best friends if your haircut is totally last century, or if you have body odor, or if that flowery shirt is just a joke. Follow their advice. Dressing in a ridiculous way can sabotage your efforts because it stops potential partners from engaging with you in the first place. But after you've done a bit of cosmetic adjustment, think about brushing up all the qualities you have to offer that are beyond the physical. It may seem hard at first, but remember, you have control. Here are some suggestions.

- Confidence is attractive. Pinpoint the qualities that make you unique, interesting, and worthy, and focus on them. Clearly define what you have to offer the world, as well as a future partner, and your confidence will radiate like a beacon of light.
- Passion is attractive. Live your life with purpose and intention. Take up hobbies you've been meaning to explore. Develop your skills and expertise. Do things that bring you real fulfillment and joy.
- Conversation is attractive. If you aren't the best communicator in the world, make an effort to polish your conversation skills and practice them continually. The best conversationalists engage others and make them feel good about themselves. Instead of trying hard to make other people feel that *you* are charming, try to make them feel that *they* are charming. That's the key.
- Optimism is attractive. If you tend to be more of a glass-half-empty person, take stock and shift your outlook. Negativity breeds negativity. The reverse is true as well.
- Good listeners are attractive. Listen intently and show a genuine interest in others. Tune into them. Refer back to something they

told you earlier to prove that you were listening. This is a very powerful tactic that is often neglected.

When it comes to finding lasting love, these tools will be far more useful to you than a new haircut or a hot outfit, and they will have benefits far beyond finding a new relationship. Focus on increasing your appeal from the inside out—because it's the inside that you want your next partner to fall in love with.

Establish who you are now

At the end of a long relationship, sometimes it's hard to remember what life was like before—or, worse, what *you* were like before. Members of a couple often stop thinking of "me" and start thinking of "we." Once you're left to your own devices again, you need to revive your sense of self.

This is one reason why it's advisable to have recharging time between relationships: not just to lick your wounds, but also to rediscover what makes you tick. A major life change, such as the breakdown of a relationship, can be an opportunity to make the changes you've wanted to make in your life, and improve the aspects that you're not happy with. Whether you want to get back in touch with old friends, learn a new language, or train for a marathon, you can create a new routine that's all about you.

Once you stop looking for someone to fill the void from your last relationship (more on this in chapter two) and, instead, are ready to find someone with whom you can share your already full life, you're ready to start dating again. Get the ball rolling by answering the twenty questions below, to pinpoint who you are and what you are looking for the next time around.

Write a few lines in your dating notebook in response to each of the following questions:

1. Who is the most important person in your life, and why?

2. What is the one dream for your life you most look forward to achieving?

3. Which person has the capacity to make you angrier than anyone else in your life? What, in particular, do they do to make you so angry?

4. Who has the capacity to make you feel loved more than anyone else in your life? What, in particular, do they do to cause you to feel so loved?

5. How do you feel about yourself—physically, emotionally, mentally, and spiritually?

6. When do you feel inspired? How does it feel when you are inspired?

7. What is the most important thing in the world to you?

8. If you had one day to live, how would you want to spend it?

9. When do you feel most afraid?

10. If you could accomplish only one thing during the rest of your life, what would it be?

11. What bores you? Why?

12. How important is money to you? How much time do you spend thinking about it?

13. What is the role of God in your life? Do you believe there is a God, and if so, what is God like in relation to you?

14. What three interests are you most passionate about?

15. Who is your biggest enemy, and precisely how and why did this person become your enemy?

16. How important is food to you? Do you feel disciplined when it comes to eating?

17. Does the idea of being married to the same person for the rest of your life sound appealing to you—or not so appealing? What is there about it that you would especially like or dislike?

18. Do you consider yourself emotionally healthy? In what ways are you especially healthy, and in what ways could you possibly concede that you could use some improvement?

19. Do you argue very much with the people closest to you? How does it usually turn out?

20. What specifically would you like your closest friends to say about you at your funeral?

If someone could hear your answers to these questions, they would come to know you well. But, of course, it's most important that you understand yourself. If you ponder these questions thoughtfully and honestly, you're sure to gain a wealth of insight that will help you to find a person who loves what you love and values what you value.

CHAPTER TWO

What Went Wrong the Last Time?

When you are going back to dating again, it's a good idea to turn the spotlight first on your own dating history, rather than on potential new partners. You want to find out why it didn't last, so you can avoid making similar mistakes again.

Just because a relationship ended, doesn't mean it was a "failure." It worked for a certain period of time and then it stopped working. Some things worked well and others didn't. By treating it as a learning experience, you can reap the benefits of the investment you made.

THE MANY ASPECTS OF RELATIONSHIPS

Many things impact a relationship. Some are obvious ("We were terrible at supporting each other"); others are more difficult to see ("Work stress made it hard to fight fairly"). As you look back at what worked, and what didn't work, in your last relationship consider:

- What role did you play in the success or failure of the relationship? You may want to believe that all the problems in your relationship were caused by your partner, but that just isn't true. You also had a role in making the relationship work, and not work. Were you overly suspicious and nagging your partner at every turn? Were you slow to provide emotional support when times were hard? Did you withdraw from the discussion every time your partner wanted to resolve a difference?

- What role did your partner play in the success or failure of the relationship? You probably see many flaws in your ex, but it is important to take an honest look at their strengths and weaknesses. No partner is all bad (or all good) and understanding what qualities your partner had that impacted your relationship will help you find the ones you need in your next partner.

- What things did you and your partner share (or not share) that made the relationship work? Sometimes the most important thing is what you share with your partner. Research has shown that couples who have similar personalities and values are more satisfied. Did you and your partner agree on religion, how many hours to spend at work, and how best to discipline your children? Which of these differences were the hardest to negotiate in your relationship?

- What stressors did you face? Stress is the big enemy of a relationship. When you are stressed it is harder to support your partner, resolve conflict, or see the good things in life. But worse than that, stress can cause us to blame our partners for things that weren't their fault. Think about the sources of stress in your last relationship. Did you have to work two jobs just to pay the bills? Were your in-laws always interfering in your marriage? Did you live in a part of town that was noisy and dangerous?

There are usually lessons you can take from every relationship, but to do this you need to look a little deeper than the obvious blame game.

- "He had an affair."
- "She nagged me from dawn till dusk."
- "He worked long hours at the office and fell asleep in front of the TV the minute he got home."
- "She talked more with her girlfriends than she ever did with me."

None of these statements is especially helpful. They may describe some of the symptoms of the issues you had in your relationship but don't necessarily help you understand the cause.

> *Four key things affected your last relationship: you, your former partner, the interaction between you and your former partner, and what was going on in your lives at the time.*

Now take it a level deeper and think about how each of those four areas impacted your relationship.

- "I was a workaholic and wasn't prioritizing the relationship." (*you*)
- "She wanted me to be more successful/more focused on the home." (*your partner*)
- "We stopped being able to communicate about what was important to us." (*the interaction between you and your partner*)
- "We both lost our jobs and fought about money all the time." (*life circumstances*)

Now you're getting somewhere. There are always many causes when a relationship breaks up. Simply blaming your partner, or taking sole responsibility yourself, will prevent you from seeing how many factors could have contributed to the breakdown of the relationship and how you might prevent those factors from recurring in a new relationship.

Take it a stage further still and think about how you might use these lessons. For example, if your last partner's expectations of the relationship differed from your own, did that make it easier or harder when times got tough?

If you don't work to understand each other, normal life problems, such as family trauma, or debt, or illness, highlight any existing weaknesses or incompatibilities in the relationship. If the relationship isn't fundamentally strong, these external triggers will open up a fault line and the cracks can widen until they are insurmountable.

One business insolvency or the death of one partner's parent might not crack a solid relationship, but it could put a lot of strain on an already shaky one. Understanding what happened in your past relationship gives you valuable information when you set out to find a better partner next time.

> *Stress can affect any relationship, but the strong ones will have more resources to cope and survive.*

Getting another perspective

Sometimes it is hard to see all of the problems that developed in your last relationship. Although you have great insight into your own experience, you are also very biased about why the relationship ended. A third party (or parties) can help you see the issues you may not have seen, or highlight how an issue you didn't think was important was actually central to the ending of your relationship.

If you did some relationship therapy during the break-up, this may have helped you to see what went wrong and why, but if you didn't, you might need to ask for feedback. A number of studies have shown that friends and family are better predictors of relationship outcomes than the individuals in the relationships themselves.

Third parties can give you a different kind of self-reflection than the one you have yourself. Their opinions may be a little more balanced than your own views of the relationship. Be prepared to hear some harsh truths. And keep in mind that your friends and family are biased, too. However, their viewpoints can help you sift through your past relationship, so are worth soliciting.

- "You never used to let him finish a sentence without interrupting." (*you*)
- "You were the fun one; we always thought she was too boring for you." (*your partner*)
- "Neither of you could cope when the money got tight." (*the interaction between the two of you*)
- "Your family/friends were always trying to undermine your relationship. Looks like it worked." (*life circumstances*)

Listen and learn. Their feedback could be a good starting point for working out what went wrong.

Next, think about the criticisms your partner leveled at you toward the end.

- "You were always in my face about something."
- "You made me feel whatever I did was wrong."
- "You never wanted to go anywhere or try anything new."

No doubt, there is a hefty dose of anger and resentment, but you may also find clues to what made your partner unhappy. It might be something you need to change about yourself before you start dating again, or it could be that your partner just wasn't the right one for you. The more you understand this, the more you can apply those lessons to your next relationship.

Take whatever you think is useful and mix it with your own instincts and you could be on the way to understanding what happened.

Now, let's start taking a look at you and your relationship patterns. Your relationship style can have a big impact on how satisfying your relationships become.

Styles of attachment

When you think of your past relationships, what did you worry about? This may sound like a strange question, but it has to do with your sense of security or insecurity in relationships.

- Some people are fundamentally secure about their relationships. They have a healthy amount of self-worth and believe that their romantic partners are generally caring, dependable people.
- There are other people who are very anxious about their relationships. Deep down, they feel as if they are unworthy of a relationship or a caring partner and are never quite sure why a partner is responsive. They are constantly worried about how much their partner loves them or whether they will find someone better and move on.
- Still others feel as if they don't need relationships. They don't believe that other people are dependable in a relationship and they would rather be on their own. Consequently, they tend to avoid relationships and commitment and will generally be detached and a bit self-centered when they are with a romantic partner.

Do any of these scenarios sound familiar?

> *Psychologists refer to these three attachment styles as "secure," "anxious," and "avoidant."*

In reality, it isn't quite that simple. We will all be secure in relationships sometimes, anxious at other times, and avoidant at still other times. But most people are closest to one style, which determines how they behave in relationships most of the time—and that can make a big difference to how the relationship turns out.

Secure behavior

Those who have a secure attachment style have a generally positive view of themselves and of other people. They think they are worthy of a relationship and that others will treat them pretty well. Secure individuals are confident that when they really need their romantic partner for support or reassurance, that partner will be there and can be depended upon. So they only turn to the partner for support when they really need it; they don't search for constant reassurance and they don't continually pressure their partner to show love and support. They also don't overreact to stressful situations and are able to step in and offer valuable support to their partner during tough times.

Think about what this means for the other partner and the relationship. Someone dating a secure partner will not feel as though they have to take care of that person all the time. They know, too, that if they need help or support, their partner will be there for them. Additionally, a secure partner is happy to display their love and comfortable when those displays of love are returned. Those with a secure attachment style are less likely to get jealous or possessive, without very good reason, which, in turn, reduces the other partner's worry that they will leave the relationship for someone else.

Anxious behavior

On the other hand, those who have an anxious attachment style don't have a very good view of themselves. They don't feel worthy of a relationship and have a very difficult time understanding why or when a partner will display love. They are not confident that the relationship is going to last, so they constantly test it to make sure it is solid. They are likely to feel threatened and jealous, and express it in poor ways. Because they are unable to handle stress well, when a partner comes to them for support they are more likely to get overwhelmed and offer support that isn't helpful.

Now think about what this means for the other partner and the relationship. Someone dating an anxious partner has to keep assuring them that they are important and wanted. Anxious partners are constantly displaying their love and need displays of affection showing that this love is returned. They are sensitive to rejection, because it confirms their self-view that they are not worthy of a relationship, so they are much more likely to take an innocent comment, tease, or joke as an indication that they are not loved. And when the other partner needs support, because an anxious partner often gets overwhelmed by those needs, it is likely that the anxious partner will be the one in need of support.

HIGH DRAMA

Some people need constant signals that their partner cares about them, and will create drama in order to get that affirmation. This can make for a very turbulent relationship, which can be emotionally draining. Just as our immune systems weaken when more demands are placed on them, constantly testing a relationship weakens and eventually wears it out. A secure person doesn't test a relationship, so its strength is reserved for times of genuine stress.

Avoidant behavior

Those who have an avoidant attachment style don't have a very good view of other people. They believe others are not likely to love and support them, and they are unlikely to display love and support themselves. They typically won't seek support, even when they need it, and will withdraw when others request it of them. Deep down they want a relationship, but they believe that displaying love will only make a partner turn away. They think the only way to keep a partner around is to maintain a degree of emotional distance.

Now, think about what this means for the other partner and the relationship. When trying to talk with an avoidant partner about feelings or worries, they will likely shut down, leaving the other partner without the help they need. An avoidant partner will consider themselves first, and be less likely to think about how to make the relationship work. They won't consider the other person's needs or try to make them feel important.

A SELF-FULFILLING PROPHECY

The extraordinary thing about attachment styles is that they can start a self-fulfilling prophecy.

- Secure people believe that their partners are dependable, so they don't stress as much about the relationship and are therefore more likely to offer good support when it is needed.
- Anxious people are worried that they aren't worthy enough so they constantly seek attention and love. Anxious individuals are more likely to pick up on the times when their partner does not provide support and interpret it as a rejection. Their typical response is then to seek even more affirmation.
- Avoidant people don't want to show love because they believe it will make others reject them. They withdraw when their partners need support.

These are extreme examples, but you can see how your beliefs about relationships can make you act in a way that insures those beliefs will come true.

Is this ringing any bells for you? Read on.

The anxious/avoidant stereotype

A common pairing is an anxious woman getting involved with an avoidant male. She seeks reassurance, and the more she does so, the more he moves away. They have selected partners who reinforce what they think of themselves. As the avoidant man distances himself in response to her neediness, he "proves" to her what she already "knew"—that she is not worthy of a relationship. The more she tries to engage her avoidant partner, the stronger his tendency is to withdraw. The behavior of each confirms the beliefs of the other.

Unfortunately, this pairing of an anxious woman and an avoidant male tends to lead to an unhappy but relatively stable relationship. It goes in line with societal expectations that women are anxious while men are detached, and confirms what both partners believe about themselves. If it's the other way around, and you have an anxiously attached man and an avoidant female, that is the least happy of any combination because it goes against the societal norm, which can magnify the unhappiness.

A relationship between two anxiously attached people would be a very passionate, volatile one, with lots of demands for ever-bigger gestures of love. They are likely to argue a lot as they constantly seek proof that the other person loves them and wants to be with them. Long term, this dynamic is likely to become emotionally draining for both partners.

Two avoidant people are unlikely to get together in the first place. They are the ones who have to be pursued and persuaded to enter a relationship at all. There usually needs to be one non-avoidant partner for them even to make it to a first date.

If you suspect you had a problematic pattern in your last relationship, it is important to recognize it so that you can try not to repeat it the next time.

You may or may not recognize your own tendencies in these descriptions. Often, we don't even realize these ingrained behaviors, nor do we consider how they may be impacting our relationships with the people we love.

Relationships tend to be more stable and satisfying over the long term when at least one member of the couple has a secure attachment style. Over time, the secure partner can help an anxious or avoidant partner become more secure because of their consistent, reliable responsiveness.

One way to minimize turbulence in a relationship is to date a secure person, particularly if you are not. You can usually tell quite quickly when you've met someone who is secure, because they don't check up on you all the time, they are able to have emotional conversations and be honest about their feelings, and they are generally emotionally supportive and available when you need them to be.

For those of you who are secure but end up with a person who is anxious or avoidant—don't worry too much. It may mean a little more drama or a little more difficulty pulling the other person out of their shell, but in the end, secure people tend to remain secure.

There are many different ways in which anxious/avoidant self-fulfilling prophecies can manifest themselves in relationships. In the next section, you'll find some examples, along with advice on how you might change those patterns, if any of them seem familiar to you.

Self-sabotage

If you are anxious or avoidant, it can lead you subconsciously to sabotage new relationships from the start, either by choosing the wrong kind of person, by choosing the right one and driving them away, or by making yourself unavailable in some way. Basically, the relationship never has a chance to get off the ground—you've made sure of that. Here are some of the ways this can work.

Choosing someone unavailable

We all want to be loved, liked, and desired. When you enter into a new relationship, you open yourself up to another person and take a risk that they might not like everything they see. If your sense of self-worth is not strong, you take all criticisms to heart and rejection makes you feel even worse about yourself. Any negative feedback is likely going to reinforce your avoidant behavior.

By choosing someone who is unavailable (perhaps already married), or who lives hundreds of miles away, or who is otherwise totally unsuitable (for example, he hates your family or she has three kids and you hate children), you have a built-in excuse for the relationship to fail. When it does, you don't have to blame yourself quite so much. But because the failed relationship reinforces your perception that you are "bad" at relationships, you are more likely to make the same poor choices again.

Do you have a pattern of long-distance relationships, or picking partners who are already involved with someone? Could it be that you are subconsciously sabotaging your relationships from the start because you are anxious or avoidant? The solution isn't always easy but admitting you have a problem is a big step forward. If your fears about relationships are deep enough, you may need to see a professional. But you can also work to break your patterns by picking partners who are more likely to be available and supportive.

Fearing rejection

If you tend to hide behind an emotional wall you've set up for yourself, you will have a hard time maintaining a successful long-term relationship. Most people aren't afraid of intimacy *per se*—they're afraid of being hurt or rejected. They protect themselves by avoiding emotional conversations and freezing out their partner in arguments. The more you shrink from intimacy, the more your partner will feel rejected and start to move away from you, and you will have yet another self-fulfilling prophecy.

The solution? If you have a fear of intimacy, you aren't likely to overcome it quickly. But learning to be honest about your feelings and asking your partner for help should enable you to work through your fears over time. You may have to force yourself to respond to emotional overtures and fight your way through feelings of acute discomfort along the way. But being conscious of your patterns and understanding why you created them is the first step to changing them.

FEAR OF INTIMACY

Some people are hypersensitive to rejection and so attuned to it that they actually expect it and see signs of it where none exist. So when their partner calls and says they have to work late, they will interpret it as rejecting behavior—"If my partner cared enough about me, they would make the effort to get home on time."

Perhaps they suspect an affair, or at the very least a cooling of passion. Their suspicion and doubts subtly undermine the relationship over time, then the rejection they feared happens, and the prophecy is confirmed.

People who fear intimacy try to shield themselves from rejection by holding themselves back in their relationships. But this just undermines the partnership even more and makes the anticipated rejection come sooner. To break the pattern, you first need to understand it and then consciously force yourself to behave differently.

Being hypercritical

When you commit to someone else, you become accountable for their feelings and needs as well as your own. Many people find that scary. Instead of being able to say outright what is worrying them, some partners become overly critical, blowing up every minor flaw in the other person and making it into something much bigger than it really is. She doesn't floss her teeth every single night? Gross! What other aspects of her hygiene might be lacking? Soon, you'll be thinking of her as a walking Petri dish of bacteria.

The solution? Try letting go of your fear and open up to your partner about it. Ask for their help to resolve it. Realize that "Commitment" doesn't mean you are responsible for every last aspect of your partner's life, from their health to their finances. They are still an independently functioning human being.

Recognize that your new partner is bound to have faults—no one is perfect—and that if you keep searching for the "perfect person," you will always fail. Keep being hypercritical, and you'll end up alone, with only yourself to criticize.

(There's more on the "C word" in chapter eight.)

Too busy to look for someone

Some people construct their social and work situations in such a way that they are unlikely to meet anyone new. If you stay very late at work and fill your leisure time with solitary pursuits, or ones that prevent you from stepping outside your normal social group, then you are making it much more difficult to find a partner. Could it be that you are doing this deliberately? Many people do, without even being aware of it. You're sabotaging a potential relationship by never giving yourself an adequate chance to start one.

If you love being single—there's no one to wag a disapproving finger when you make an extravagant purchase, no one to check in with before accepting an invitation for drinks after work—then that's just fine. But in that case, why are you reading this book?

If you want to meet someone but it's just not happening, have a look at your lifestyle and ask yourself if you are undermining your chances of finding love. If this is the case, make the decision to rearrange your priorities and start taking active steps to meet new people. There are lots of suggestions about how to do this in chapter five. Whether you are the CEO of a huge corporation, or a single mom with five kids, you can find an hour to spare to join an Internet dating site—and that could be all it takes.

Too picky

If you have such a long and detailed shopping list of demands to be met in a new partner that it would be virtually impossible to fill them all—sorry, George Clooney and Salma Hayek are already taken—then this is another form of self-sabotage. You need to be prepared to be realistic in your search or you will never find a partner. Ask yourself if you have identified so many requisite qualities in a partner because they are all truly important to you, or because you are afraid of being hurt again. By being "picky" you avoid ever having to put yourself in that situation.

There's a lot of advice in chapter four about choosing the main qualities to look for in your next partner, but you may need to be prepared to trade off some of them. For example, if you want a very attractive, successful lawyer, you need to realize they will probably have to spend a lot of time in the office working rather than at home canoodling on the sofa with you.

Think carefully about whether your pickiness is really defensiveness. And if it is, be brave. Follow the advice in chapter four and come up with a more realistic (and shorter) shopping list.

Andy and Julia

Andy had had his heart badly broken and he was wary of getting involved with anyone else. He just didn't think he could take another pounding if it all went wrong again. He came home every night to his two cats, Harry and Sally, who were complete characters and always made him laugh.

It was safe, staying behind closed doors. But after a while, he really started to miss the emotional and physical closeness that come with being in a romantic relationship.

Eventually, Andy realized he didn't want to end up a sad, lonely old person with noone to live for. He joined a dating agency, but not without trepidation. The possible heartache was never far from his thoughts.

When he met Julia, all of his fears went out the window. She was such a warm person that he felt safe and happy with her from early on, and they never looked back. The cats liked her as well, as if more proof were needed!

How to break your relationship pattern

If you now realize that your avoidant or anxious behavior may have contributed to your last break-up, it's time to take steps to change before you repeat the same cycle again. Avoidant and anxious types need to understand that in their responses to their partners, they are making their worst fears self-fulfilling. They are confirming their own negative stereotypes. The more often they do, the more the behavior will become entrenched.

If this pattern is deep enough, you may have to conduct a deeper analysis of the reasons for your behavior. It could have roots in your childhood or past experiences. This can be very difficult to do on your own, and it can be painful once you start, so consider consulting a professional counselor or therapist to help you through the process.

TALK THERAPY

There are many different kinds of talk therapy available, and they all use different methods. If you think childhood trauma is at the root of an entrenched behavioral pattern or way of viewing the world, a psychoanalyst could take you back through it in a safe environment and help you to come to terms with the trauma and move on. In cognitive behavior therapy, you won't analyze the past but will learn specific techniques for coping with situations you find difficult. Person-centered counseling, gestalt therapy, and transactional analysis, among others, help you to learn to feel good about yourself and develop in a positive way. See page 216–217 for advice on choosing a therapist near you.

Past hurts and fears, whether from childhood or from more recent relationships, weigh us down and make it difficult to start new and healthy relationships. That's why lots of self-help books talk about "unloading baggage."

Baggage is all the negative feelings of anxiety, depression, anger, fear, and resentment that you may be carrying around without even being consciously aware that you're doing so. You could meet a really great person with whom you are deeply compatible, but your baggage could stop you from seeing them in a realistic light and forming a healthy relationship. You might be overly avoidant and put up barriers against intimacy, or you might be overly anxious and end up driving them away.

Letting go of your baggage is not as easy as unloading a suitcase from an airport carousel. Certainly, some types of hurt, anxiety, and depression will get better with time, or you can resolve them yourself with a little self-reflection. Below we go over some steps on how you can start that process. But there are other issues that are much more difficult to deal with because they are so deeply seated—things like having been physically or emotionally abused, or past problems with substance abuse. These issues require professional help and you should be very wary of trying to address them yourself.

If you feel able to look at your own "baggage," try following these five steps.

Step One: Ask yourself a few good questions

Shaking off memories involves dealing with inner conflicts that may have left you feeling vulnerable from a miserable event or set of events. Sometimes it's hard to pinpoint, but you'll notice baggage creeping up in unexpected ways. The key is to take your time and assess your individual issues thoughtfully. Use the following list of questions as a starting point. Write up your answers in your dating notebook.

- Where did you grow up?
- What was it like being a child?
- What were your mom and dad like?
- Can you identify the impact on you of any parental dysfunction?
- Have you ever felt out of control in your adult relationships?
- Have any dysfunctional relationships with siblings, ex-partners, or friends had an impact on you?
- Did they foster self-doubt or anxiety about yourself?
- Are you overly sensitive to anxiety or depression in other people?
- What are the things that you think are most damaging to your romantic relationships?

Now rank these issues according to which are the most traumatic and difficult for you to deal with. These answers are a starting point for you to consider how your past relationships may negatively impact your current relationship. Remember: you may not be able to see all of these issues for yourself. Don't be afraid to talk to a trusted friend or family member to see if they agree or have a different point of view.

Step Two: Write about your issues

Now that you have a list of issues that are traumatic for you, start to write about them. Describe what those issues are, why they occur in your life, and how you think they affect your ability to form and maintain satisfying relationships. Write about how you think you might be able to address these issues. Devise a plan of action to make the anxiety and pain you feel from them lessen and eventually disappear. Just keep writing whatever comes to mind around that issue.

Chances are, the act of writing about a problem will help you work toward a resolution. Writing therapy can be more effective than talk therapy, as it can help you to organize your thoughts and ideas, which in turn can help you pinpoint what the problem really is and how to move past it. It might seem odd to write about your problems like this, but try it. It can be very effective!

Step Three: Understand the source

The act of writing and self-reflection should eventually help you understand the root source of your problems. This might have been the death of a beloved caregiver when you were a child, or rejection by an early crush, or even something you caused by your own actions. If the source of your issues feels overwhelming and you can't see a way to deal with it yourself, it's time to seek professional help for your problems. However, it may be that with the passage of time since the event in question, you feel able to set it into some kind of perspective that will help you to deal with the emotional repercussions it caused. In cases where you did have a hand in creating the problem, own up to your own faults, and don't be afraid to face them. If it wasn't your fault, try to accept this once and for all. Understanding is a great big step in the right direction.

Step Four: Lightening the load

As you come to understand the source of your problems, you may start to see ways of resolving the issue. If you are lucky, merely acknowledging the issue may allow you to get rid of that excess baggage. But more likely, you will realize it will take some time to work thorough your feelings. Writing can be helpful in this process.

Gradually, your mindset should begin to change and this will alter the way you experience the world. As you start to react differently, other people will behave differently toward you. There's a domino positive effect. Once you build your own self-esteem, others will somehow sense it and they'll behave more respectfully around you; when others are treating you well, you feel even better about yourself. Much like the securely attached individual, once you start to expect that you deserve a good relationship and that others are dependable, you will start to behave in ways to confirm that expectation.

Step Five: Step out in faith in the present

Once you have addressed your issues and changed your expectations (i.e., "let go of the baggage"), you will start to notice the world treating you in a different way. You may have other issues that you need to address and it may take some time. But once you find yourself starting to believe you are worthy of a relationship you will be in a position to control your fate, rather than believe that the world, or chance, is controlling it for you.

Try selecting a partner who is different from those with whom you had poor relationships before. Remember: you are trying to overwrite patterns that may have been engrained for many years.

• If you were always dating people who were unavailable, find someone who is ready for a relationship.

- If you always ended up with people who were high drama, search for someone who is lower key.
- If you realized that you were sabotaging relationships, make yourself face those unproductive behaviors.
- If you were clingy because you were insecure about your relationship, plan nights when you *don't* see your partner so you can learn that time apart does not mean the other person has lost interest.
- If you always wanted to run away whenever your partner came to you for emotional support, take a deep breath and go to *them* for emotional support.

These behaviors will feel very uncomfortable at first, but should help you change the way you think about your relationship.

Over time, as the relationship becomes more settled, you will naturally start to feel more secure. And if you choose a partner with whom you have plenty of core values and traits in common (see chapter three), you'll have a much higher chance of success, which should help to build your confidence even more. In the back of your mind, always try to recognize your patterns of avoidant or anxious behavior and correct yourself if you feel you are slipping backward. Secure attachment behaviors can be learned. The more you practice, the more comfortable and happy you will be in your relationships.

BEYOND VIOLENCE

If your last relationship was violent and abusive, it's important that you deal with any issues in your past that may have caused you to fall into that kind of situation. You will probably need professional help to do this. There are organizations that can help listed on page 216–217. In a new relationship, you will have to watch very carefully to ensure that you don't fall into any similar patterns again.

Are you ready to meet someone yet?

After a break-up, whether it ends in divorce, bereavement, or mutual agreement, there needs to be a period of grief and adjustment before you dive into dating again. If you are still emotionally affected by the past relationship, you will be difficult to be around and won't attract the kind of person who will be best for you when the good times return.

It takes a while to recognize the lessons you need to learn from a relationship, and usually we can't see them until the immediate emotional consequences are past. The length of time this takes will vary from person to person, but it should always be roughly proportional to the length and importance of the relationship you are emerging from.

- If you were married for twenty years and your spouse died suddenly in a car accident, you're going to need a significant amount of time before you are ready to date again.
- If you were in a year-long relationship that didn't get all that deep—you never considered marriage—then the time to get over it should be much less.
- But grieving for six months over a relationship that only lasted two weeks is a sign that there are some deeper issues going on for you. Maybe the break-up pressed some triggers that reactivated old childhood grief. You may need to get professional help to deal with these past traumas effectively.

People who are secure get over relationship break-ups more quickly than people who are anxious. An anxious person can end up mourning for an inappropriately long time before seeking another relationship to fill the hole left by the last one. That new relationship is unlikely to work because they are approaching it with unhealthy or unrealistic expectations.

WHEN A NEW RELATIONSHIP IS NOT THE ANSWER

Entering a relationship in the hope of finding someone to help you get over past traumas creates an unhealthy dynamic from the start. Examples of this could include looking for a parent figure if you feel you need someone to look after you, or looking for a healer if you want to be "fixed." In both these instances, the qualities that attracted you to the other person would become irritating to one or both of you over time, as the parent figure persists in telling you what to do, or the healer becomes a doormat, sublimating their needs to yours. The solution is to fix yourself before going into a relationship so that you make healthy choices at the outset.

In the immediate aftermath of a relationship, people might experience signs of depression, such as changed sleeping patterns, trouble concentrating, feeling worthless, or feeling guilty. They may become overly agitated, or very tired, and have a severe loss of interest in things they used to enjoy. For some people, this period of depression will last two weeks, for some it's four weeks, and for others it's much longer. (If these symptoms last for more than a few weeks, consider talking to your doctor, who can help. They may advise counseling, or extended treatment, or perhaps a professional listening ear will help.)

Depression is a natural part of getting over a relationship, so you need to go through it and take care of yourself until it passes. There's no way you should even consider looking for a new relationship during this period, because you'd be going into it for all the wrong reasons. You'd pick someone who made you feel temporarily better, without any consideration for the relationship over the long term.

The gray area comes once the overt depression has passed. Are you ready to move on or not?

As long as your major focus of attention is still on the emotional consequences of the last relationship, starting a new one will be difficult.

Do you still talk a lot about your ex? Are their photos still on display in your home? Are you still wearing a wedding or engagement ring? Do you brood over mementoes of your time together? All these would be signs that you have lingering issues to resolve.

If you were married, you should try to deal with every last practical issue related to the marriage before you try to get involved seriously with someone new. Because divorces are extremely painful, many people delay dealing with paperwork or financial issues. To give a new relationship the best chance of succeeding, you need to start with the slate as clean as possible. Plus, it isn't fair on your new partner if you are still working through issues with your ex.

Do you feel "hot emotions," such as fury, toward your ex? You don't need to give them a full pardon for everything that occurred between you. But you do need to stop carrying around the baggage of your anger, or it will put a real damper on the chances of the next relationship succeeding.

DANGER SIGNS THAT YOU ARE NOT READY TO MOVE ON

- Hair-trigger defensiveness: you have vowed never again to let anyone treat you as badly as your ex did, so you jump disproportionately at the slightest hint of a recurrence of certain behaviors. When someone you are dating irritates you in some way, stop and ask whether you are behaving appropriately or if your response is supercharged with old emotion from a past relationship.

- Do you "trash-talk" about your former lover? Under the guise of sharing details with a new lover, you are lifting the lid on a simmering stew of resentment and pain. This is not attractive. Better to let go, cool down, and wait until you are genuinely ready to move on.

- If a new date shows any similarities to an ex, no matter how innocent, you hear alarm bells and get ready to run. This is misguided, because your ex is bound to have had some good qualities that you should look for in your next partner. It is fine to be wary when a new date shows similarities to your ex in terms of qualities that made the relationship go wrong, but if you are reacting to harmless similarities, you may not be ready to start again. The trick is to shed the incompatible aspects of the last relationship but keep the ones that worked.

Be honest with yourself about this. You want your next relationship to be a really healthy one, so don't minimize any lingering feelings you have for your ex or issues that you still have to resolve. Work through them completely before getting involved with anyone else—for their sake as well as your own.

If you have childen together you still need to be in contact with your ex, but it will benefit all of you if conversations can be civil and calm. There's more on this in chapter nine. Screaming matches on the doorstep are obviously unhealthy, but conversely staying "best friends" with your ex can be problematic as well, making it difficult for a partner to fit in (see page 158 for more on opposite-sex friendships). No one forgets the past, but we can all learn from it and eventually use it to reconnect with the world as a wiser person.

Lisa and Colin

Lisa's two teenage daughters watched her struggle for ten years after getting divorced from their father. Not only was it hard being a single parent, but when Lisa's father became ill they had to move into his house so she could take care of him. These were difficult years, culminating in her father's death at the end of a tough winter for everyone.

Lisa's daughters kept urging her to "get out there" and start dating. She knew they had her best interests at heart, but the time was wrong for her. She was grieving for her father and was just in a bad place. She had to get through her mourning, and decided to focus on being a good mom.

In the summer of the following year, Lisa's daughters saw a commercial on television for a dating site, and they registered on their mom's behalf. She was initially shocked when she found out what they had done, but when she thought about it she realized she was ready to give it a try.

Lisa was put in touch with Colin. She knew she was onto a good thing when their first phone call was two hours long They had so much in common that they couldn't stop chatting, and what's more they seemed to be looking for the same things in life. They are now married and haven't looked back, but Lisa believes that if she had met Colin even a year earlier, she wouldn't have been ready for a relationship. The timing had to be right.

CHAPTER THREE

Compatibility Explained

Relationships begin in all sorts of ways. Your eyes meet across a crowded bar; two friends decide one night that there could be something more than friendship going on; he comes to install new windows and you just get to talking...

In Western society, physical attraction plays a large role at the start of a relationship. If you are single at a party, you don't generally look around and think: "Oh, I want to meet him because we clearly have so many shared interests;" or "I think I'll go and talk to her because our values are so obviously the same." We tend to believe that without at least some level of physical attraction, a good romantic relationship cannot happen.

Research shows that we will spend more time looking at someone we find attractive, and we are more likely to forgive their faults. Physical attraction makes us want to touch, kiss, and have sex, which all promote intimacy in a relationship. A relationship just isn't the same without that buzz.

Movies and television help to propagate this idea. Our celebrities are almost perfectly attractive, and we have crushes on them. Romance in Hollywood movies almost always starts with overwhelming physical attraction and chemistry (and usually succeeds against all odds). Television commercials encourage people to spend thousands of dollars trying to make themselves look younger and more attractive. All of these things send the same message: only the physically attractive will be desired.

But physical attraction is only one part of the complex balancing act of a good relationship. In the long run, partners who sacrifice compatibility for physical attraction and chemistry often end up unhappy. Many traditional cultures around the world understand this and choose to use family matchmakers, who will look at the personalities, tastes, beliefs, and family backgrounds of the people they are matching to try and pick a couple who they think have the right qualities to make each other happy long term. If physical attraction follows, that's great, but it's not essential.

In Western society, we tend to look for physical attraction first. This sometimes makes us try to shoehorn the rest of that person into the kind of mold we want them to fit.

ARRANGED MARRIAGES

Friends and relatives can be objective matchmakers because they are not caught up in the throes of passion. Usually partners in arranged marriages are chosen by familial or community elders who presumably know the individuals well and can determine who will be a good long-term fit for them. Within a particular set of cultural circumstances, arranged marriages have shown to be very successful.

But arranged marriages can backfire when people match for the wrong reasons. Quite different are "power marriages" in which, say, the King of France marries the Queen of Spain for financial and territorial advantages to their countries. History is littered with the debris left in the wake of such mercenary arrangements!

Right now you are probably saying to yourself, "Well, of course, you shouldn't start a relationship based purely on physical attraction! That's crazy! There are many other things you need to make a relationship work!"

You are right. Most people also want that mysterious kind of attraction known as "chemistry," which goes beyond pure physical attraction. But what exactly is interpersonal chemistry, and how much importance should we give to it?

A chemistry lesson

There are two different aspects to what we call "chemistry": physical chemistry and psychological chemistry. Physical chemistry, believe it or not, is based on your immune system—something known as "Major Histocompatibility Complex," or MHC. Unlike psychological chemistry and compatibility, when it comes to MHC, you want to be different from a partner. Sounds odd? Here's how it works.

If you want to skip the science, all you need to know is that physical chemistry is based on how someone smells and it helps couples produce healthier babies.

Our immune systems are designed to keep our bodies safe from foreign invaders. We wouldn't survive without it. When our immune system identifies a microbe or cell that isn't our own, it attacks it, kills it, and removes it from our body. This is a complicated job, because the immune system needs to recognize which cells are our own, and should be left alone; which are foreign but not dangerous (such as pollen and food), and can be ignored; and which ones are a threat (such as bacteria), and should be eradicated.

When our immune cells are not good at discerning the differences, they might attack our own healthy cells, which can lead to autoimmune diseases such as lupus or rheumatoid arthritis. If they attack foodstuffs or environmental triggers such as pollen, we suffer from allergic reactions and illnesses. If our immune systems were not good at detecting dangerous invaders, we wouldn't be able to fight off colds and flu and everyday bacterial infections.

MHC molecules help in this process by taking some of the proteins from inside the cell and moving them to the outside of the cell, where they can be more easily identified. These proteins, known as cell surface markers, signal to our immune system that this cell is not foreign or dangerous, and can be left alone. But foreign microbes, such as bacteria or cancerous cells, also have MHC molecules. If our own cells do not have enough unique cell surface markers, the immune system has trouble identifying what needs to be attacked. When MHC molecules are highly varied, we have many unique cell surface markers, and our immune system can better identify which cells to leave alone and which to attack. This makes us healthier.

So how does this affect our relationship choices?

We want our children to be as healthy as possible. And when we mate with someone who has MHC molecules that are very different from our own, the baby will end up with a stronger immune system. Scientists have discovered that we find romantic partners who have very different MHC molecules sexually attractive. This difference is probably communicated by scent molecules. For example, one study showed that women liked the smell of T-shirts that had been worn by a man with a very different MHC molecule from their own. Partners who have different MHC molecules are more likely to get pregnant, less likely to experience complications during pregnancy and childbirth, and have children that are more likely to be healthy. So this is "chemistry" at work.

But this isn't the only type of chemistry. The second type of chemistry is different from this subconscious, scent-led type of detective work.

It's interpersonal or psychological chemistry, which is driven by a very different process.

> *Psychological chemistry is what leads to two individuals feeling a connection or "click" with each other.*

When we first meet someone who attracts our interest, we are alert and picking up all sorts of clues, consciously and subconsciously, about the type of person they are. On an obvious level, their clothes and the type of jewelry or watch they wear can indicate their wealth and social status. On a less obvious level, their posture, facial expression, and movements can give away something about their personality, such as whether they are dominant characters or not, or whether they are introverted or extroverted.

We do this remarkably quickly, within seconds of meeting someone for the first time. And while we are sometimes wrong, these judgments are generally surprisingly accurate.

As we continue talking to a person who has attracted our attention, we listen carefully and continue to uncover clues about their personality. Can we trust them? What do they like or dislike? Do they value the same things? Do we have anything in common? Most of the time, understanding another person at this level is harder and more time-intensive.

When we meet someone we are attracted to we try to present our best selves, so we don't express every thought that crosses our minds, or tell tales that make us look bad. Because both people are trying to hide their bad qualities and emphasize their good qualities, it can take longer for the "real self" to emerge.

Every once in a while, the conversation is dramatically different. We find ourselves saying the same thing at the same time. There are odd characteristics you have in common—maybe a shared love of Verdi operas, or the color indigo, or watching Japanese game shows. As the conversation gets more enthralling, you ignore everything else; you lose track of time; you anticipate what the other person is going to do next. You "click."

Intimacy is about feeling understood, cared for, and validated by another person. Psychological chemistry can give an initial clue as to whether this might be possible. But it's not by any means infallible.

WHAT IF THERE'S NO CHEMISTRY?
Chemistry isn't always instantaneous. It can develop over time as you get to know a person better. But how long should you wait? First meetings and first dates can be stressful, so people often don't come across as themselves. Once they are more relaxed, you might see quite a different side to them. If by the second or third date, you can't ever imagine yourself holding the other person's hand or kissing them, you should probably reassess the situation and think about moving on. No matter how perfect they may seem in theory, if you lack that crucial spark, a romantic relationship between you is unlikely to endure.

Why first impressions can be wrong
Initial attraction to someone tends to be based on a mixture of physical appearance, chemistry (both physical and psychological), front-end personality (as displayed in the first conversation), status (as shown by clothes, jewelry, and so forth), and sense of humor. So far, so good. It's worth agreeing to a date if all these impressions are positive, but these qualities alone do not mean the relationship is going to be successful. Even if you find the other person sexually attractive, and you both like Jackie Chan movies and feel a great sense of connection, you may still find that in crucial ways you are totally incompatible.

Angela and Ray

Angela was looking for a dating service that would help her really get to know someone. When she and Ray were matched by eHarmony they had no idea what the other looked like. They could see each other's likes, dislikes and "must haves," and both felt interested enough to email with more questions. The fascination grew as they exchanged photos and began speaking on the phone. They were obviously deeply compatible, but lived on opposite sides of Australia, and were scared that when they finally met there might not be any physical attraction. But they needn't have worried. After a quick hug at the airport, they relaxed, and it wasn't long before they realized that something magical was evolving. They got married in 2005, and both of them now recommend the eHarmony system to all their single friends.

If you choose a partner based on chemistry and first impressions alone, you could find you have nothing left to talk about once you've made it through the initial honeymoon period and watched all the martial arts movies ever made. Initial attraction doesn't offer much evidence about whether your personalities, core values, and beliefs are similar, or whether you will be able to satisfy each other emotionally, or to resolve conflict satisfactorily.

In some cases, your inner insecurities and anxieties can lead you instinctively toward the wrong person, such as an "avoidant" person choosing an "anxious" person and vice versa, or someone with a troubled past looking for a partner to "fix" them, as discussed in the last chapter. It feels right to you because that's the pattern you are used to, but you need to look beyond this for someone with qualities that will help you move out of your normal pattern. (See pages 35–40 for more on how to do this.)

It's fine to use chemistry as a starting point in your search for a partner, but beware of being so blinded by lust and optimism that you don't look for signs of the true compatibility that will mean your relationship has a better chance of succeeding long term.

The truth about compatibility

There's an adage that opposites attract. This is true when it comes to magnets, where like poles repel each other, but applying this rule to your romantic pursuits can be a recipe for disaster. Forging a relationship with someone unlike you is hard, because differences require negotiation and adaptation. While these differences can be exciting at first, negotiating them over time can become exhausting. Accommodation and compromise are important in every relationship, but constant accommodation and compromise will create stress and strain a relationship, which can lead to break-ups. You might initially be attracted by someone who is completely different from you, but in the long run, those differences will make a relationship harder.

Over the last decades there have been dozens of studies showing that we are more likely to date or marry people who are similar to ourselves in terms of physical attractiveness, attitudes, and values, as well as religion, education, and intelligence. There are several theories as to why this happens.

One is that we are more likely to meet (and marry) people from the same economic class, neighborhood, university, or church. So, for some characteristics, couples are similar because similar people are more likely to live close to one another.

A second idea is that we like people who share our attitudes and beliefs because they validate our opinions. We want to believe that our attitudes are right, but can't always prove it. We might think that Italians make the best pasta, and the French have the best wines, but it's not possible to demonstrate this definitively. When we meet someone who shares these attitudes, we like them because they validate our own attitudes, values, and opinions. In other words, we like people who are similar to us because they make us feel good about ourselves.

Perhaps most important is the consistent finding that similarity is related to relationship success. However, it's not necessarily similarity in political views, or the football team you support that's most important, but similarity in your core personality traits, attitudes, emotional tendencies, and most deeply held values (for more on opposing political views, see page 70).

> *Personality traits, emotions, attitudes, and values all influence the way in which we respond to life situations.*

For example, if something bad happens to a couple, those with similar personalities will react in similar ways, signaling to each other that they both take the situation seriously and both have similar goals in resolving the situation. This lets both members of the couple show understanding for one another, which often leads to better outcomes, both for the problem at hand and the relationship overall. A couple who are not similar to start with, who react in different ways to bad news, will feel that the other person doesn't understand what they are going through and does not share their goals.

Imagine you hear a rumor at your office that there might have to be some job losses soon. You want to come home and talk to your partner about all the details you've heard, as well as speculate about who could be targeted, and even plan a way of making everyone understand that you are indispensable to the company and thus save your own job. It's at the forefront of your mind and you need to get it off your chest. You particularly want to feel as though your partner is on your side. However, if your partner is the type who mulls over decisions by themselves, rather than talking them through with others, they might not understand your need to share, and could shut you down with a throwaway comment: "By the way, I'm going to the gym this evening. You go ahead and eat without me." You would feel hurt and rejected. And your partner might not even understand why you are hurt, because they don't deal with stressful situations in the same way. It could result in a fight or a festering discontent-ment with each other that could put a strain on things over time.

This is not to say that all incompatible couples fail to stay together. There are lots of reasons why unhappy couples don't split. Some stay for the sake of children, some because they don't believe in divorce, and others because they couldn't survive financially on their own so feel they have no choice. Remember the bickering elderly couple back in chapter one? Being incompatible doesn't mean you will split up, but it does mean that you are more likely to be unhappy in the relationship. You will have a better chance of being happy together long term if you operate in a similar way, with the same set of values.

In truly compatible couples, love deepens as they go through cycles of self-discovery and rediscovery of each other. Over and over again, they fall in love in slightly different ways, reaffirming their commitment toward the relationship they share. Despite beginning in the same euphoric way as compatible relationships, incompatible relationships have a much different outcome as time marches on. Instead of falling in love more deeply, each partner falls into emotionally separating periods of resentment that mount until the pain and frustration of tolerating each other's idiosyncrasies outweighs the desire to keep the relationship going.

Compatibility can make the difference between a relationship that lasts and deepens over time, versus one that ends in emotional disappointment.

Knowing how to identify someone with whom you will be compatible is a two-part process. First, you must know your own traits, values, and the relationship skills you bring to the table—good ones and areas where you could possibly improve. Your responses to the questions at the end of chapter one should provide a clearer indication of your strengths and weaknesses. The second part of the process is learning to recognize the meaningful traits in others that go well with yours.

It's all right to have some dissimilarities between you and a potential partner; being completely the same can be as problematic as being completely different. However, the more differences you have in your personalities and values, the trickier it will be to have a strong relationship that endures over time. In looking for compatibility, there are some core traits and vital attributes that are particularly important.

Core traits
Core traits are facets of personality that are highly unlikely to change once you reach adulthood. They can be adapted to fit with another person's style to an extent, but they are the foundation of who you are as an individual. While everyone has slightly different core traits that are most important to them, there are four in particular that most affect relationship compatibility.

Emotional temperament
When you are feeling worried about something—or, conversely, ecstatic about something—do you tend to share your feelings with the world? Some people are very open and want to express their emotions, while others feel uncomfortable and withdraw from emotional outpourings. Are you more likely to feel positive emotions or negative emotions? When you experience something new, are you excited or anxious? Positive and negative emotions make you act in very different ways: positive emotions make you want to engage, while negative emotions, most of the time, make you want to retreat.

People with different emotional temperaments react differently to conflict. One partner wants to engage and talk about it, and perhaps shout or cry. The other one shuts down and moves away from the conflict, which in turn makes the first partner want to engage even more. It can turn into a pattern called demand/withdrawal (see page 148). More often, it's the woman who wants to approach and becomes demanding, while the man wants to withdraw—but this is not always the case.

NATURE AND NURTURE

Society sets women up as the caretakers of relationships. From an early age, traditional girls' games involve taking care of others, while boys are more likely to be led toward active physical play. That's part of the reason why women tend to be the caretakers of social relationships more often than men. But another theory says that women evolved in large social groups that had to cooperate and socialize to survive, while men evolved in hunting groups that were more likely to require a different form of cooperation and less socialization. This means that women may also have evolved to navigate social relationships differently than men, which may explain why they are more likely to engage in relationships actively. There is plenty of ongoing debate and research on this subject!

If you and your partner are balanced in terms of your emotional temperament, you are better able to deal with conflict down the road because you communicate your emotions in a similar fashion. In the same situation, you will be more likely to experience the same kinds of emotions. You feel comfortable in the way that you are displaying and experiencing these emotions. So, for example, two relatively reserved individuals who don't often show their emotions, or two people who are very expressive and emotionally open, will be much better matches than one partner who expresses and another who withdraws.

The more similar you are in the way that you experience and communicate emotions, the easer it's going to be for you to understand what your partner is thinking and feeling.

You don't need to have an exact match—and that would be difficult to determine anyway—but there are all sorts of areas where a fundamental emotional mismatch causes problems.

- If you are celebrating a success, such as a promotion at work, and you come home jumping up and down with excitement, but your partner just glances up from the television and says "Great news," instead of cracking open the champagne, you could feel unloved. They might be thinking to themselves "I'm really proud," but you are not hearing it.
- If you receive some bad news, say about the failing health of a close relative, and tell your partner you are feeling very sad and anxious about it, you might expect demonstrative emotional support. An undemonstrative partner could seem uncaring, even if they are actually very concerned for you.

However, even though having the same emotional tendencies helps partners understand each other, it is bad if they feel exactly the same way all the time. When one partner is feeling overwhelmed by a particularly stressful day, the other one needs to understand those feelings but still be able to remain calm so they can be properly supportive. If both partners tend to get very anxious and stressed, they will just make each other worse.

Say your partner is worrying about a meeting with their boss the next morning after some mistake has been discovered in their work. It doesn't help if you take on that worry with them and say "What will we do if he fires you? How will we pay the rent?" You need to stay calm and help them resolve problems, while letting them know that you understand their feelings. You could say something along these lines: "I know this is very stressful for you, but your work has always been great in the past, and your boss would be crazy to let such a valuable team member go."

A properly empathetic partner will be able to separate themselves from your anxiety and help you to get through the situation without becoming so upset themselves that they are overwhelmed with emotion and unable to help.

EXTREME CASES

Expressing emotions in a similar way to your partner is good except in extreme cases. If you both have appalling tempers and poor anger management skills, it's going to make for a very noisy and volatile household. If you are both verbally abusive to each other, you'll end up in a very negative, unpleasant relationship. (There's more about abusive relationships on page 40.) At the other end of the scale, two people who never express their emotions to each other could be harboring resentments for years that will explode messily at some point in the future. (See page 146–152 for more on dealing with tension in a relationship.)

So there are three parts to emotional temperament. You should look for a partner who:

• Expresses emotion in a similar way to you
• Generally experiences emotions in the same way as you
• Can help you manage your own emotions during times of stress

We'll look at ways you can assess a potential partner's emotional temperament in chapter seven.

Social style

Your social style is the way you interact with the world. If you are very sociable, constantly looking for company and conversation, then you should look for a partner who is similar, so that neither of you has to regulate your lifestyle. If one person loves huge parties with dancing and live bands playing, while the other prefers small, intimate dinner parties, then you will have to negotiate disagreements about how to spend your evenings.

At the outset, during the honeymoon phase, you might be happy to try out each other's social style. Someone who is less sociable might find it exciting to attend big flashy parties for a while; a party animal might enjoy snuggling up in front of the TV every so often. But if you are at core an introvert, you could find it difficult to form a successful long term relationship with an extrovert. Let's look at what these terms mean.

- Extroverts are outgoing, talkative, energetic, assertive, outspoken, and adventurous and tend to be enthusiastic and optimistic. They enjoy being with other people and often assert themselves in groups. You might describe them as "the life and soul of the party" or "born leaders." We all know people like this.
- Introverts are more quiet, reserved, low key, and solitary, usually with less enthusiasm and energy than extroverts. They prefer solitary to social activities. They are not necessarily shy, although they can be. They can demonstrate extrovert behaviors in a social group, but they are not entirely comfortable doing so.

Which social style do you think you are most like? How would your friends describe you? Perhaps you appear more extrovert than you feel, because you have developed social skills over the years that help you to mask underlying insecurities.

Extrovert and introvert are not rigid classifications, but people tend to
fall loosely into one camp or another, to a greater or lesser degree.
We all have a basic quality of extraversion or introversion as part of
our personalities, but it can appear in a different way, depending
on the people we are around. For example, someone might be
extroverted at work if their job is an event planner, but if they come
home to a very lively partner, they might appear more introverted by
comparison.

Their differing social styles mean that extroverts and introverts
approach relationships differently. Extroverts develop relationships
quickly, while introverts may have difficulty getting to know other
people or initiating intimacy. Once the relationship is established
and there is mutual trust, however, the introvert may put even more
effort than the extrovert into maintaining it and making it deep
and satisfying.

*Having different social styles doesn't
necessarily mean you're incompatible; it's
just an area that will require negotiation
and compromise over the years.*

Similarity of social style is important for some people and not so important for others. It really depends on how flexible you are. The partner who says "I really want to stay at home all the time" is much harder to be with than one who says "Maybe I do lean toward staying in, but I'm perfectly happy to go out and socialize sometimes as well." We all know couples that socialize separately to an extent, so that the more extroverted partner can get their fill of parties without dragging the more introverted partner along. If there's enough trust in the relationship, and they still share plenty of interests and activities together, this doesn't have to be a problem.

However, if you have similar social styles to your partner, it will be one less difference in your relationship that will require negotiation.

Cognitive mode

Your cognitive mode has to do with how open you are to new experiences, and how intellectual and thoughtful you are about the world. Both partners should share a similar level of expansiveness and curiosity about new things. If your cognitive mode matches with your partner's, you are more likely to share similar interests. That's beneficial for the relationship over time.

Having the same kind of general orientation toward the world is more important than having exactly the same interests. An intellectual person might like to read a lot, they might like to go to political debates, or to museums, which are different activities but similarly intellectual pursuits. Finding a partner with a similar level of intellectual curiosity gives you a better chance of sharing interests in the future, even if they prefer theater to politics, or bowling to tennis.

Imagine you are both browsing the news, and your partner comments on a story about how whale migration patterns are changing because of a warming of water in the Pacific Ocean. Now, you might not be interested specifically in whales or in climate change, but if you and your partner have similar levels of curiosity about the world, you will be interested to hear about this news story that has caught their attention. It might not be one that you would have picked out to share, but you can appreciate why it is interesting.

All relationships are going to have a balance between shared interests, which help to drive and give the relationship a common theme, and individual interests, which are not shared. Most couples find the balance naturally. Not many men would choose to see only movies such as the latest Hollywood romantic comedies. Women are generally less inclined to be interested in cars. You don't have to be a carbon copy of the other person, but you do want to have some interests in common that the two of you can enjoy together. There's more on this in chapter eight.

What's also important is that you are not disdainful of each other's interests. Let's say you don't like computers but your partner is a real techie. When they call you over wanting to show you a neat trick they've learned in a particular program, or a geeky YouTube clip, it's best if you can manage to have a quick look and say "Wow! Who would have thought it?" rather than retort "I would prefer to have my fingernails pulled out with pliers or watch paint dry."

Over the years, couples tend to take on aspects of each other; that's part of the growth of a relationship. Sharing new experiences together can help to keep passion strong. So being open to developing new interests together, or perhaps becoming more involved in an interest of your partner's that you didn't share at first, is a very healthy sign. And if you have similar cognitive modes, this is more likely to happen.

Physical energy
Having similar energy levels to your partner can be crucial, because it affects so many aspects of your life together. This is not just about how much time you spend on the go versus sitting with your feet up relaxing. It's also about how ambitious you are to accomplish things in

the world; how industrious you are; even how much sex you like to have.

- As you can imagine, when someone who is very interested in sex gets into a relationship with someone who is less interested in sex, it can lead to conflict that they will have to negotiate. There's more about this in chapter seven.
- If you are an athletic, energetic, outdoorsy person, while your partner is a bookworm, you will essentially end up leading separate lives.
- If you feel that you are always the one picking up the vacuum cleaner and taking out the trash, while your partner sits with their feet up, the day will come when you can't bite back the sarcastic comments.
- If you work hard to earn extra money, move up the career ladder, and create a nice home for your family, you might start to resent a partner who takes the morning off work to sunbathe in the backyard.

Fortunately, energy levels are relatively easy to discern. You should be able to tell in the early weeks of a relationship whether someone is compatible with you on this level by the type of dating activities they suggest, as well as the hobbies and interests they enjoy.

LARK VERSUS NIGHT OWL
We all have different body clocks. Some people are at their most energetic and creative in the morning, while others don't get going until after noone then want to party late into the night. It's not necessarily a relationship killer if you are a lark and your partner is a night owl—you'll just have to negotiate. Maybe you can enjoy an hour or so of peace in the morning while your partner sleeps in, and you can have an early night while they watch the late movie.

Brenda and Mark

When Brenda was matched with Mark he was serving with the army in Baghdad, so their courtship was online for several months. They were so amazed by the number of similar interests and tastes they shared that they began to wonder if there was some kind of experiment taking place with them as guinea pigs. For example, she mentioned that she was taking a new job and he replied that he lived 500 yards away from that office. For his birthday, Brenda put together a package of different things, and she decided to include some Skittles candy. She always liked to separate the colors before eating them, so she did this almost automatically. She emptied the large bag into a bowl, put each color Skittle in a small plastic bag, replaced all the little bags in the large one, and resealed it before closing the box and mailing it. Two days later, when they were emailing each other on the subject of "little known facts about Brenda and Mark," he mentioned that he liked Skittles but only ate them one color at a time. Brenda was amazed. Her package couldn't possibly have arrived already. She checked and it hadn't. It wasn't the kind of core trait or value that eHarmony talked about, but how could she resist someone with similar candy habits? They're married now and Mark has adopted Brenda's daughter.

Vital attributes

Your vital attributes indicate the life experiences you have had and what you have learned from them, as opposed to the personality you were born with. It's nurture rather than nature. Compatibility in the following three areas will help the future success of your relationship.

Your backgrounds

You don't need to have been born and brought up in the same hometown, or have attended the same college, or have a similar number of siblings for a relationship to work. Sharing these factors doesn't necessarily breed success in a relationship, but it does breed commonality: a shared set of assumptions about the world that means you have less to explain to your partner.

If you come from a markedly different cultural background from your partner, you are likely to have to explain all kinds of issues and customs to each other throughout your relationship. Those from different countries, even continents, will celebrate different festivals—Diwali in India, Burns Night in Scotland, Thanksgiving in the US. They may have different attitudes to family, with some expecting elderly relatives to live with them, rather than retirement homes. All these matters would have to be explained and negotiated.

A high-school dropout need not be the intellectual inferior of someone with a Ph.D., but unless they are extremely widely read on their own, they won't have the same set of reference points as someone who has been through higher education. They might feel out of place at a dinner party with their partner's colleagues if they don't share the same breadth of general knowledge, and that could lead to tensions in the long (or short) run.

Coming from a similar type of family to your partner can be very helpful, because it will be more likely that you share the same kinds of ideals on issues such as child-rearing, discipline, and family bonding. This can be especially important in second-time-around relationships where one or both of you may already have kids. How are you going to amalgamate two sets of kids who have been brought up with different styles of discipline? The ones who were less disciplined will resist being more heavily disciplined all of a sudden, or those who used to be more disciplined might go crazy with fewer constraints. Advice on bringing two families together is in chapter nine.

PERSONAL HABITS

In a long-term relationship, compatibility in your approach to personal hygiene and domestic habits can become important once the first flush of lust and romance has faded. It's going to be a growing source of irritation if one partner is obsessive-compulsive about housework, while the other is happy to let the dishes sit around for a day if there's something more fun to do. Personal habits such as table manners, tidiness, or not putting the soap back in the soap dish are details you may be willing to overlook at first. But they can become real sources of aggravation later. You might end up feeling a disproportionate sense of anger every time your partner picks their teeth after a meal, or leaves toenail clippings on the bathmat. Watch out for these kinds of incompatibilities early on and see if they can be nipped in the bud before they become huge issues.

Do you want to have any children together? This is, of course, a million-dollar question when choosing a new partner. Don't assume you will change the other person's mind down the line. Once you get back to dating again, you have likely made up your mind whether or not you want kids.

After having a baby, does the woman expect to be a traditional stay-at-home mom? It's amazing how many couples don't even talk about this in advance of conception, because they make assumptions based on their own backgrounds. But if a traditional type of woman gets together with a man who thinks women should be more independent, then there is going to be a problem at some stage.

And yes, money does affect compatibility to an extent. If you have been brought up in a mansion with servants, it's challenging to switch to a small apartment with no help. People's attitudes about money are often formed in childhood, and this will affect matters such as whether they tend to run up credit card debt or budget every last penny, whether they scrutinize every bank statement, or just have a rough idea how much is in the account at any given time. Incompatibility in those areas can be a major source of tension, as you can imagine.

The more background attributes you have in common with a potential partner, the greater the chance of having a relationship that will withstand the challenges of time.

Relationship skills

The skills we use in our relationships, such as conflict resolution, managing emotions, and effective communication, aren't set in our DNA. They can be improved. For example, if one partner is significantly better at negotiating conflict, the other can pick up their techniques. If both partners are poor at negotiating conflict, that's not so promising. There's advice about conflict resolution once you're in a steady relationship in chapter eight, but at the outset, try to work out whether you and your potential partner have similar styles. When you argue, do you both blow up, let it all out, and laugh about it minutes later? Or do you sit down for a calm, rational discussion.

Men may be from Mars and women from Venus when it comes to communication, but, even so, they must share a general level of verbal intimacy skills to have a rich and rewarding relationship. The ability to be honest about thoughts and feelings is a very good sign in a potential partner. Conversely, people who bottle up their feelings and don't give any hints when they're annoyed about something are very difficult to be with.

Knowing when to use humor, and having compatible senses of humor, is a big plus. If you are standing on the kitchen floor with water up to your knees from a burst pipe and the baby is crying in the next room, you may not feel it's the best time for a joke; on the other hand, you might appreciate someone lightening the mood. It's an individual preference.

Having the ability to engage the other person in conversation is another important relationship skill. When you are relating an anecdote, can you pick up the signs that the other person has lost interest and move on? Or do you continue regardless, determined to reach the punch line? When you are listening to someone else, do you let your mind wander to what you are preparing for dinner, or remind yourself to mail a letter? If your conversation skills are much better than your partner's, this could become irritating. Then again, they may improve as they learn from your good example.

In the early stages of a relationship, most people will be trying hard to communicate effectively. Then they may get lazier over time. Keep listening and you will pick up clues that will help you determine your long-term compatibility.

Values and beliefs

If you are very religious and go to church every week, say grace before each meal, and pray every night, it can be problematic if your beliefs are not shared by your partner. They are not engaging in something that you feel is very valuable and important to you. Interfaith relationships and marriage can work if both partners share roughly the same level of spirituality and commitment to their religion. If they are a confirmed non-believer, it may feel as though they are denigrating the very heart of your faith. If you have children together, how will you raise them? Will they go to a faith school or not? Will they be brought up to believe in your view of the universe or your partner's?

There are degrees in all things. If your beliefs are less important—a kind of backdrop that doesn't impinge much on your lifestyle—then they need not be so crucial in your choice of partner. But be prepared for some difficulties time and again; for example, when planning a wedding or dealing with bereavement.

There are plenty of couples that vote differently during elections and have differing political views. Despite being aligned with different parties, you may find these couples have many shared views and philosophies. But extreme political differences between partners are more often problematic in relationships than not. Every time a news item comes on TV about budget cuts for the homeless, or a tightening of immigration law, or tax breaks for big businesses, there's a potential for an argument.

Once again, it depends how deeply you hold your convictions. If you are running for political office as a liberal, it may feel like a real betrayal if your partner contributed money to a right-wing candidate and hung a poster endorsing the opposition candidate in your window at home. But if neither of you is especially politically engaged, you may get away with differences. Few couples agree on every single aspect of government policy, just as few politicians agree.

How traditional are you? Do you idealize living in a nice home with a family, taking a couple of vacations a year? Or would you rather live in a cabin in a forest, foraging on the land for food? Do you want to take a sabbatical to sail around the world, or would you rather stay in your own neighborhood among a close network of friends and family?

How altruistic are you? How much of your income do you give to charity? If you keep separate checking accounts, this need not affect the relationship unduly, but with a joint account you will need to agree. How willing are you to help friends in need? There could be crises down the line if you are the type who is happy to let a friend crash on your sofa for a few weeks after a relationship break-up, while your partner resents the intrusion.

Are you ecologically friendly? If you recycle every last vegetable peeling in an effort to save the planet, while your partner drives a 4x4 to the corner grocery store, you're going to have clashes at some time.

Once you get past your teens and early twenties, your values and beliefs become an inherent part of your identity. Before choosing a partner, identify the things you value most—your core values—and choose a partner who is able to understand them and share most of them.

Not just like you

You are a unique human being and it would be impossible to find someone who is exactly like you. When estimating your compatibility with someone else, think of each major area where you have different core values or vital attributes as a withdrawal from a bank account. Each area where you agree is a deposit. If the balance is high, you can afford more withdrawals. But if you have many vastly different opinions and attitudes in major areas of life, your balance is going to become dangerously low. Over the years, the continual need for negotiation and compromise in your relationship can bankrupt your account.

ADAPTABILITY

There's a crucial ingredient that can make every part of a relationship more stable, and that is adaptability. This quality acts as a buffer zone between you and serious problems. It can't make up for significant differences in core values and vital attributes. But even if just one partner is adaptable, the relationship can often "work." This doesn't mean you should become a chameleon, taking on your partner's colors and shedding your own. But recognizing the power and benefits of compromise is a fantastic skill, and one that can be nurtured and expanded in your relationship.

In chapter four, we'll be looking at how to choose the qualities in a partner that will be most likely to make your next relationship stronger and healthier so you have plenty of "cash in the bank."

CHAPTER FOUR

What Do You Want in a Partner?

We all grow up with fantasies about the person we would like to spend our lives with. These could come from fairy tales, which make little girls yearn for their very own handsome prince to slash through a hundred-years'-worth of overgrown briar hedge and rescue them and by the early teens, most of us probably saw our ideal type as being like our favorite singer or movie star.

Some people get stuck in this kind of fantasy, looking for a perfect mate who lives up to their ideal. This may be why some men only date models, and some women date sports stars, in pursuit of their own particular dream partner. We've all done it in one form or another, and often with the same result—disappointment. Why?

Because no one can live up to the image we've built up in our heads. Once you realize that the ideal person doesn't exist and move on, you are that much closer to finding a happy and healthy relationship, one that's real and solid rather than head in the clouds.

HANDSOME PRINCES

You may have a visual image of the handsome prince or princess you want to meet, what they do for a living, where they live, and how old they are—but it's time to put away the superficial checklist you've created over the years and approach finding a life-long partner with fresh eyes. Remember, you are looking for someone who will make you happy in twenty years' time, when the sparkling blue eyes might be a little less sparkly and the perfect skin etched by laughter lines.

In this chapter, you are going to create a list to help you define more clearly what you are looking for in your next partner. It won't be a hard and fast, "break one rule and you're out" kind of list, but it will help to focus your thoughts on choosing someone with whom you will be compatible and will therefore increase your chances of making a relationship work long term.

"Must haves" and "can't stands"

In your dating notebook, make a list of the ten qualities that you want your next partner to have. This should include practical issues as well as core traits and vital attributes, and it should cover the following:

- Do you need someone who is kind and supportive?
- How far are you willing to travel to start a relationship?
- How young is too young?
- How old is too old?
- Do they need to want to have children with you?
- Can they already have children? Do they need to accept that you have kids?
- What are the most important characteristics for you to share with a new partner?
- Do they need to be religious (or not religious)?

Refer back to your answers to the questionnaire at the end of chapter one, and look through the core traits and vital attributes in chapter three to help you choose your ten "must haves".

AGE MATTERS

In most heterosexual couples, the woman is slightly younger than the man; this trend persists even in the 21st century. Most men still marry younger women and most women marry older men. The biological reason is that the couple will have more time in which to reproduce before her fertility declines—but this comes at a cost. At the other end of life, men tend to die younger than women, so she will have longer on her own.

Age gaps are less of a big deal as you get older. The ten-year age difference between fifty-five and sixty-five is not a problem, but between eighteen and twenty-eight it is too big most of the time. More importantly, at any age, if there is a generation between you, you might find that you have grown up with different core values and sets of assumptions, which will require some explaining and negotiating. It can work, but it's harder. See page 93 for more on choosing the age group of partner you are interested in meeting.

Coming back to dating the second time around, you have a big advantage over those who are starting out, because you know what worked for you the last time as well as what didn't work. You have a clear picture of your "must haves" and "can't stands." The first time you go into a relationship, it's harder to judge in advance what you really won't be able to live with, but the second time around this should be much clearer.

If your last partner drove you insane with their messiness around the house, you might be best advised to look for someone neater.

Every time a new partner left a jacket draped over the back of the sofa, it could summon up bad memories and put you on edge. Similarly, if your last partner had a pun for every occasion, you may have had enough of stand-up comedy. Much more seriously, if your last partner was abusive, you will want to be sure that your next one is a gentle, caring type who is able to control his or her emotions (see page 40 for more on this).

Now choose your ten "can't stands."

- If you had a bad experience last time, you may be tempted to list lying, jealousy, or infidelity here.
- Include any bad habits, such as smoking or drinking excessively, that you simply couldn't live with.
- There may be some physical or aesthetic traits that are a "no-no" for you, such as obesity, bad teeth, or a terrible dress sense.
- List any core values that would be completely at odds with your own and that you think would cause conflict, such as low levels of ambition or a lack of emotional empathy.
- Write down any vital attributes that you couldn't stand to differ on. These might include religious beliefs, or not being a good conversationalist.

It may not have been easy, but you should now have two lists with ten items in each. However, it is probably unlikely that you will find an individual who can check all twenty boxes for you. It is rare, and maybe impossible, to find that perfect partner. Everyone has to make trade-offs. So the next step is to look down your two lists and think about which items are the most critical and which you would be willing to give a little ground on. Strike out the ones you can let go of most easily.

Even with this shorter list, you may still have to make some trade-offs, so now rank the importance of the remaining items. It will help you keep in mind what you are willing to trade off, what is absolutely critical, and what seems critical, but you can live with (or without).

Dean and Sue

For Susan, the decision to get back into the dating game was a long process. Four years after separating from her ex-husband, she had only a limited social life. She went clubbing very occasionally, but one thing she was sure about was that she didn't want to choose her boyfriend when under the influence of alcohol. This wasn't how she chose her clothes and it wouldn't be how she chose her man. After making the decision to join a dating site, she sat down and thought hard about what it was she wanted back from a relationship. She wanted someone to listen to her when she'd had a bad day at work. She wanted someone to share a joke with over a meal, someone to love her for who she was, and someone whom she could love unconditionally in return. When she started speaking to Dean she knew instantly that he matched her values and general outlook on life, and they hit it off right away. Seven months after their first date, Dean got down on one knee and proposed, and Susan was one hundred percent sure he was the man she had been looking for.

"Must haves" versus "really prefers"

What if you met a person who was perfect in every way except that they were a smoker, and you can't stand smoking? Is that enough to rule them out? What if they are five inches shorter than you would prefer? Or if they like a glass of wine every night and you don't like to drink?

Researchers have identified some qualities that are critical, perhaps even necessary, for a relationship to work. For example, someone who is an Orthodox Jew is unlikely to have a successful marriage with a Buddhist. When these core values and characteristics are shared, that couple is much more likely to be satisfied.

Other things, such as height, smoking, or weight are preferences. Although couples tend to match on these characteristics (tall people tend to marry other tall people; short people tend to marry other short people), sharing (or not sharing) these characteristics doesn't necessarily impact the quality of the relationship. Two people who have very different religious views are unlikely to be happy in a relationship with each other, but there are plenty of couples where one is very short and the other very tall who are extremely happy with each other. It just depends on personal preferences.

Unfortunately, almost every partner will have a characteristic that you don't like. Many people go into relationships thinking: "Oh, they will change for me," or "I can make them change." Smoking is a case in point; your partner may be able to give up smoking, but don't bank on it. If you assume that you will be able to change them and they will give up the butts, you may be disappointed and frustrated; addictions can be very deep-seated and hard to break free of.

Rather than going into a relationship asking yourself whether you will be able to change the other person, you should ask: "If that quality does not change, do I still want to be with this person? Can I accept that this is part of who they are?" If it is something like leaving a coffee cup in the sink without rinsing it, pressuring the other person to change would probably create more problems than learning to live with this small flaw. Clinical psychologists call this Acceptance Theory.

Every partner is going to have some qualities you won't like. If you want to be with them, you will just have to accept the qualities you don't like but won't be able to change.

Decide which of the items on your lists are preferences and which are truly critical.

Some people become pickier as they get older. They wouldn't consider anyone with children, or someone who doesn't earn a six-figure salary, hasn't been to college, doesn't like the novels of Ernest Hemingway, and is not interested in keeping tropical fish. They may well have higher standards when it comes to practicalities than they would have had when they were twenty. For example, if they have achieved a certain standard of living, they don't want to end up subsidizing a penniless dreamer.

Wide divergence in salaries is more of a big deal when the woman is the high earner; in Western society, many people still aren't used to the idea of the woman being the main breadwinner and would feel uncomfortable in that situation, although this is changing fast. Other people are completely comfortable with this set-up (see page 180–181).

When you set rigid guidelines regarding characteristics such as hair color, body type, and size of bank account, you are placing an emphasis on preferences and at the same time drastically limiting your pool of potential partners. Like the hemlines of yesteryear, what works now may be totally different from what you sought out years ago. Reconsider how much his career, her marriage history, or someone's fashion sense really factor into the success of a relationship. Bear in mind that as you mature, your needs and wants will continue to evolve and change, just as they have changed from when you were fifteen to where you are now.

Now look at your lists of "must haves" and "can't stands" again and strike out the least important until you have two lists with three criteria each. That's right—just three. You want to consider the widest possible range of candidates in the first instance and narrow the search later. Don't let a real gem slip through your fingers because of some rigid adherence to a list.

GEOGRAPHY

Long-distance relationships are stressful. They're not impossible, but they are much harder to negotiate. Relationships get stronger through shared experiences, shared duties, and building a home together, and if you are not doing much of any of those things, the partnership won't evolve. The early, heady euphoria may last longer, because of the continual separations and reunions, but strain will show over the long haul. Research indicates that if you have already established a solid relationship before you start to live apart, then it is much more likely you will last than if you start off living hundreds of miles apart and try to get to know each other in snatched weekends and late-night phone calls. If you fall for someone long-distance, you'll have to be prepared to put in extra effort to make it work. Modern technology such as Skype can help to keep the phone bills down, and you can sometimes get cheap travel deals if you book in advance and choose off-peak travel times. But in general, the closer, the better, is a good rule of thumb.

When you are cutting down your lists, remember the following:

- Physical attraction is important at the beginning of a relationship, but by itself it won't make for a satisfying long-term partnership. Don't sacrifice sharing a critical core value because someone is "hot."
- Couples' interests tend to merge over time, so even if he doesn't care about contemporary art or she doesn't appreciate vintage wines right now, their interests in these areas might develop over time, as they come to learn more through exposure to your enthusiasm. Personality and values don't change as much, so you need to pay more attention to them at the beginning.
- Someone's approach to money is much more important than how much they have, especially when there isn't much. However, more money tends to make things easier, because it removes some of the stress of having to worry about paying the bills.

- If having children is important to you, how far would you want to go in your efforts? Are we talking IVF, egg donation, sperm donation, surrogacy, or adoption? Is it the be-all and end-all, or could you live without children if that's the way the cookie crumbles?
- There are different ways of measuring intelligence, and academic success is only one of them. Some qualities are subjective and can only be judged upon meeting someone and spending time with them.
- Look at your "can't stands" and think hard about whether they would really matter in the right person. Picking your nose is not an endearing quality, but if everything else is perfect, maybe you would end up finding it kinda cute. It takes all kinds...

On every issue, think about how much you could adapt and which would be the deal breakers, the ones you really couldn't compromise on. Then take your list of three "must haves" and three "can't stands" and move on to chapter five, where we will think about ways in which you could meet the type of potential partner these lists describe. In chapter seven, we'll look at ways of assessing whether a person meets your specifications and is likely to be compatible with you long term.

Lisa and Kevin

Lisa glanced at Kevin's online profile but decided not to contact him because he lived 158 miles away from her, which was just too far to commute, especially since she had a daughter from a previous relationship to look after. However, somehow, as she scrolled onto the next page, she accidentally sent Kevin what the site called "an icebreaker," which was basically a nudge to let him know she was interested. He replied, they were both online at the time, and before she had time to start worrying about the distance, they'd sent several emails back and forth, which convinced her that she wanted to meet him. They had a record seven-and-a-half-hour phone conversation before he drove down for a date with her, and they haven't looked back. They are now engaged and she and her daughter will soon be moving to the area where he lives.

CHAPTER FIVE

Looking for that Certain Someone

When you are dating the second time around, you'll find that many of the arenas you used in your teens and twenties are now closed. In school and at college you were surrounded by people your own age, most of whom were single and looking for a partner. Now, most of your friends are likely to be in relationships, and many workplaces discourage office romances. When you attend a party, the percentage of single people, which might have been 80 percent in your teens, could have dropped to 8 percent or less by age forty.

How many single people do you know? Make a quick list. Why not join forces with them to pool your ideas about good places to meet other singles in your neighborhood? It may turn out you already know people among you who have the potential to become romantic partners.

> *There are 104 million unmarried Americans over the age of 18—that's 45 percent of the population. Not all of them will be looking for relationships, but plenty are.*

The next thing to do is increase the possibility of meeting someone new. There are countless ways to do this, requiring varying degrees of effort, but all of them require you to change your routine to an extent and take some chances. For a start, you'll have to start hanging out in new places if the old ones haven't been producing results.

If you are honest, you can probably think of a recent opportunity you didn't take advantage of because it would have swept you outside your comfort zone. Maybe it was the chance to join a salsa class, to have coffee with a friend of a friend who wanted advice about your industry, or to do some charity fundraising. Promise yourself that the next time something that will allow you to meet new people comes along, you will grab the chance, no matter how unlikely it seems that it will produce dating results. Now is the time to start taking risks again.

In the very first chapter of this book we talked about how having an internal locus of control made people more likely to take action and more likely to be successful in finding, creating, and maintaining a relationship. Even if it doesn't feel comfortable taking control of your dating life, rather than waiting for love to find you, it's going to make it much more likely that you will find that special someone.

The person you could fall in love with is out there, but unless you try hard, you might never meet them. Isn't that alarming? If you live in an urban area, there could be a thousand unattached people living within a ten-mile radius, and surely at least one of them would be compatible?

However, relying on your own and your friends' circles of acquaintances is going to narrow the odds of you meeting someone new. There are plenty of single people your age but, like you, they don't go out as much as they used to, so that narrows the odds even more. You might be lucky, but you might not be. And wouldn't you rather be more in control of your own future?

Andrew and Jessica

Andrew and Jessica met online and started emailing each other. He mentioned that he had grown up in Woodridge, Illinois, and was startled when she said that she had as well, because both lived in Atlanta, Georgia, by then. It seemed quite a coincidence. In a whirlwind of emails comparing notes, they realized they had attended the same small school, were in the eighth-grade band together, and had been members of the same church. The coincidences and connections grew until they opened their eighth-grade yearbooks and found a photograph of the two of them standing shoulder to shoulder. They had barely known each other back then, but knew a lot of people in common. They're married now, but they wouldn't be if they hadn't taken steps to connect. The moral is that even if you grow up down the street from the man or woman of your dreams, you can't rely on love finding you—not without a little help.

Read the "ways and means" list opposite, and promise yourself to try at least two of the strategies suggested in the next month. If they don't start producing results, add another method every month until you are meeting plenty of potential partners and have started dating.

Some of these may seem odd to you, because they may not even have existed the last time you dated. Remember: you have to meet people to start a relationship, but not every meeting will turn into a relationship. So go into these with a sense of fun and adventure. Even if you don't meet someone special, you could end up with some new friends and many fun nights out.

Just be sure always to follow the safety advice on page 109 when arranging a date with someone new.

WAYS AND MEANS

- Organize a singles' party. Find a location. Ask each of your single friends to bring two or three of their own most eligible single friends. Add music, food, refreshments, and turn the lights down low.
- Ask your friends' partners if they know anyone single who might be suitable for you. If so, they could either arrange a blind date for you both, or invite that person along to a social event you are all attending.
- Social networking sites, such as Facebook and Bebo, are proving to be great new ways of meeting a partner. Reconnect with your old friends, some of whom may also find themselves single, or may know someone they can introduce you to.
- Look back at the key interests you identified in the chapter one questionnaire. Join a society relating to one of them. It could be a book club, an architectural association, a gliding club, a wine-tasting society, or some kind of night class or course.
- Art galleries are good places to meet single people. The approach might be tricky, but you clearly have something in common.
- Try singles' dinners, where groups of single people try out interesting restaurants in the vicinity.
- Volunteer to do charity work, fundraise for a political party, help out at your local church, join a choir, or join some kind of professional networking group.
- Take up (or revive your interest in) a sport such as tennis, golf, or sailing, where you can join a club that organizes social as well as sports activities.
- Drag your friends along to some new bars and clubs you haven't tried before, so you can check out the scene there.
- Traveling on your own to an interesting location (Everest base camp, the Costa Rican rainforest, Angkor Wat in Cambodia) is a surefire way of meeting new people. You'll always find yourself talking to strangers when you go off the beaten tourist track. (cont'd)

- Look into singles' vacations. Many of these offer an opportunity to learn a new skill, such as regional cooking, diving, yoga, or screenwriting, so you'll have plenty to discuss with your companions at the end of the day.
- Newspaper and magazine personal ads don't give you much information to go on, but most let you call and listen to a recorded message, or provide links with an Internet profile.
- Speed-dating may seem a little odd, but it can introduce you to many people very quickly and help you to work on your first-impression skills.
- Join the millions of people worldwide who are already Internet dating: 19.4 percent of singles in the US and 25 percent of UK singles already do it. Choose between photo-based sites and matchmaking sites. There's more about this on pages 91–102.
- If you are daunted by computers and want a more individual service, there are agencies that will personally match-make to your specifications. This tends to be expensive, but is worthwhile if you don't have much time or want to be sure your anonymity is maintained.

Conquering hesitancy

What are you afraid of? If you are hesitant about putting yourself out there and admitting that you are looking for love, then ask yourself why. Is it because you are proud and think it is in some way a failure to be single? Are you worried about colleagues teasing you? Is it because you have security worries about meeting strangers? There are answers to all of these concerns.

First of all, a sense of shame about being single is *so* last century. There was social stigma attached to getting divorced pre-1970s, but now it is a normal part of life. It happens. Which of the following fictitious women would you find more admirable?

Janet

Janet was in a ten-year marriage, which ended when she was thirty-three years old. She knew she wanted to have children and that her biological clock was ticking loudly, so she threw herself into dating as if it were a second career. She joined dating agencies, answered personal ads, signed up on social media sites, asked all her friends to help, and she started dating, and dating, and dating. At times, she dated as many as three men in one evening, and fifteen in a week. She had a couple of short-term relationships, but she moved on as soon as she was sure they weren't going to work long term. It took her four years, but she finally met Chris when she was thirty-seven. They dated for a year before deciding to try for a baby, and she got pregnant at the age of thirty-nine. They are now happily married and have a son and a daughter.

Katie

Katie was also in a marriage that ended when she was in her thirties, but she didn't want to try online dating or singles' events because she thought they would make her look desperate. She is a stunning, sexy woman with a sunny personality who never has any problem attracting men who meet her. She continued to date men she met through her normal social circle, and she never turned down an invitation to a party, but she soon found she was being invited less frequently. A lot of her married girlfriends were too insecure to introduce such a gorgeous single woman to their husbands and preferred to meet her for girls' lunch dates instead. She is still single in her mid-forties, but maintains that her "certain someone" is out there somewhere and that it's only a matter of time before she finds him.

Katie could be single for a very long time if she continues to wait for Mr. Right to find her, but imagine what she could achieve if she started being more proactive in her search for love? There's all to gain and nothing to lose.

Stop hesitating and start trying the "ways and means" you feel most comfortable with, and then take stock after a few months. Are you getting results? If not, is it because you are too shy to ask for a date? See the advice below. Or are you doing something that puts people off? Check out the advice on first date behavior in chapter six. Or is it the case that despite your best efforts, you are still not meeting enough single people to choose from? Consider adding more "ways and means."

Meeting in a non-singles-oriented environment

When you meet someone you find interesting in a situation that is not specifically singles-oriented, you need to do a bit of detective work. Are they wearing a wedding ring? Are they gay or straight? Where do they live? Does anything about their conversation indicate whether or not they are in a relationship?

You could slip in a question that assumes they do have a partner and wait for them to contradict you. For example, if you've been talking about waterskiing, you could ask: "Does your partner go waterskiing with you?" If they say they don't have a partner, then you can proceed to the next stage.

Watch their body language (for advice on this, see page 112–115) and try to judge whether they are feeling the same way you are. The clues will be there. Before you have to go your separate ways, try to find a way of getting some contact details or arranging another meeting. It will feel most natural if this suggestion can arise from a common interest you have been discussing.

- "If you give me your email address, I'll send you a link to that great website I was telling you about."
- "Would you like to meet for coffee some time and I'll lend you a copy of that book I mentioned?"
- "If I can get tickets for the play I told you about, would you like to come along with me?"
- "You said you like Martin Scorsese. Why don't we go and see his new movie next week?"

Or just be direct:

- "You seem really nice and I'd like to take you for a drink some time."
- "When are you going to ask me out?"

Whether they are interested or not, no one could fail to be flattered by such an offer. Confidence is attractive. What have you got to lose?

ASKING FOR A DATE

If you want to ask someone you have already met (but don't know well) for a date, keep it light. Don't suggest a weekend in a romantic cottage right from the outset, or you could come across as scarily intense. Try to pick up on clues about how interested they are in you and respond accordingly. There's advice about reading body language on pages 112–115.

Meeting at singles' events

The key when attending a singles' event, whether it's a party, speed-dating, singles' dinner dates, or singles' vacations, is to approach everyone you talk to as a potential new friend, rather than as your next spouse. Don't treat it as a job interview where you have to reel off your résumé, and don't subject them to an intensive interrogation about their job prospects and life plans. Just chat and see if you like the other person first. Maybe it will turn into a friendship rather than a romantic relationship, but that's no bad thing. Every new friend you make increases your social circle and the number of invitations and introductions you get.

- Make eye contact and smile.
- Listen to what they have to say and ask pertinent questions.
- Don't tell endless anecdotes about yourself, but be open and friendly in response to their questions. If you sense you're talking about yourself too much, steer the conversation back to the other person by asking: "Has that ever happened to you?"
- It's fine to talk about the "singles' scene," or the success (or otherwise) of the particular event you are attending, but don't let on if you've been trying singles' events for years without any success!

If you decide they are an interesting person, then you can consider whether or not there's enough chemistry to suggest an actual date. One of the good things about meeting at a singles' event is that you know you are both looking for a partner, so that's one hurdle out the way. Ask if they would like to exchange email addresses so you can stay in touch. If you're sure you like them, you could suggest meeting for a real first date. There's lots of advice on handling first dates in chapter six.

BLIND DATES

If friends offer to set you up on a blind date with someone, it's always worth trying, because you surely must have something in common to have a mutual friend. Follow the first date advice in chapter six. Don't get your hopes up too high, though, because there is no accounting for chemistry. If it doesn't work out, don't take it personally and jump to the conclusion that your friend doesn't know the first thing about you: "How could they think I'd go out with someone like that?" Remember: they were only trying to be helpful—and one day it might work.

Online dating

The world of dating has changed over the last decade, and if you
don't date via the Internet these days you are putting yourself at a
huge disadvantage in comparison to those who do. But still, some
people have objections to it, or worry about how it would work.
Below are responses to some of the most common queries.

Q: **"But what will we tell people who ask how we met?"**

A: You could, if you wish, choose the place where you had your
first date, and say, for example, "We met in a coffee bar." But
by the time you are telling your grandkids how you met, they
will be astounded that anyone ever met in any other way
besides the Internet. "Really? There was a time when you just
waited to bump into people socially? How weird!" Being
honest about how you met will show other people that you
are a proactive, open-minded, and modern individual.

Q: **"Wouldn't I be at risk meeting complete strangers
like this?"**

A: You're at less risk than if you meet someone in a bar when
you've had a few drinks, especially if you follow all the security
advice on pages 100–102.

Q: **"What if my colleagues at work see my online profile?
Or clients I work with?"**

A: Find a matchmaking service that only shares your photograph
with the people you are matched with, or a dating site that will
allow you to keep your photograph hidden until you choose to
let someone see it. You don't need to give your full name, the
name of the company you work for, or any details that would
identify you until you are comfortable with the person with
whom you are in contact.

If you still feel unsure about online dating, you're acting like those people back in the 1980s who vowed they would never use mobile phones because they didn't want to be accessible all the time, or those in the 1990s who refused to use the Internet because they thought it could expose their computers to viruses. Most of us can't imagine living without either now. Online dating services have come a long way from the early days, and you'll find there's a site tailored to you whatever your criteria and needs. Close your mind to it, and you are closing your eyes to a vast pool of potential partners.

On average, 542 people who met on eHarmony get married every day in the U.S.A.–and that's just one agency.

Getting started online

There are all kinds of dating sites out there. Some are very general and aim to appeal to everyone, while others are more specialized. There are dating sites for Christians, Jews, Muslims, and Mormons. There are gay and lesbian sites. There are sites for farmers, doctors, lawyers, athletes, and even sites for "beautiful" people, in which other members get to vote on whether or not you are good-looking enough to join.

How can you choose between them? One of the main distinctions is between photo profile sites and matchmaking sites, like eHarmony. On photo profile sites, people are selected primarily on the basis of their pictures. If you want to meet a lot of people, go on a lot of dates, and have some fun, then this could be for you—but remember, if you are looking for a long-term relationship, there are many things you need to know about a potential partner beyond what they look like. Some of these are not easy to see on the surface. For a more scientific method of finding a long-term partner, though, it makes much more sense to choose a full matchmaking service, like eHarmony, where you can find someone whose interests and values match yours.

Matchmaking websites perform a service similar to a very good traditional matchmaker but websites have a pool of tens of thousands of potential matches to choose from (while an individual matchmaker would be lucky to have fifty).

If you have chosen to use a matchmaking site, the next step is to answer all their questions about your personal preferences. Remember not to be too picky. Try to keep your age range nice and wide. One of the great aspects of Internet dating is that your non-negotiables, such as children, religion, and location, are out there in the open from the start.

CHOOSING AN AGE RANGE

You will be asked about the age range of partner you want to consider. Keep it as broad as possible, so as not to rule anyone out for the sake of a year or so. There's no particular rule of thumb, because a person's goals in life are more important—but, obviously, if you want children, age is significant. If you are an active seventy-something who wants to travel, you might not want to partner with an eighty-year-old with limited mobility. Women over the age of forty can be at a disadvantage on photo profile sites, where a lot of men look for someone much younger than themselves, but if you use a website such as eHarmony, the majority of people are looking for a serious relationship based on shared interests and values, so age is less important.

It's always best to be honest in the information you give, because you will feel more at ease when you meet someone for a first date. By giving a false description, you could be wasting your own time and that of your date. There is evidence that people are prone to increasing their height by an inch on average, reducing their weight by roughly seven pounds, and chopping two or three years off their age. These might seem like small lies, and may not be a big deal if you are only going to date a few times, but what if you find a potential long-term partner and they happen to catch sight of your passport six months or a year down the line? They'll wonder what else you've been lying about.

After answering the questionnaire, you will then be asked to write a profile of yourself. This represents what you're all about and what you're looking for in a mate, so it has to be as good as you can make it. Put in some time, effort, and, most important of all, thoughtfulness when writing your profile. Remember that hundreds, maybe thousands, of people will be reading it. Here are some tips.

- A bit of humor is good, but if every sentence contains a joke, it will sound as if you are trying too hard—especially if your jokes aren't all that funny.
- Honesty is good, but avoid self-deprecation, which can come across as depressive.
- On the other hand, no one likes a braggart.
- Remember that people can't always "hear" when you are being ironic in a written piece and may take what you say literally.
- Be cheerful and upbeat. Whatever you do, don't start listing the reasons why your previous relationships haven't worked, and don't provide a grocery list of all the bad things in your life.
- Don't try to be too clever, or you will alienate many more people than you'll attract.
- Don't be overtly sexual—which comes across as provocative—unless you are looking for a purely sexual relationship.
- Mention your hobbies. Why not talk about what a perfect weekend or a perfect vacation would entail for you? These are fun things that also give people a sense of who you are.

- Use your computer's spelling and grammar check programs to make sure you don't include basic errors. You'd be surprised by how many people overlook a profile based on misspellings, bad grammar, and "text talk."
- Try to sound friendly and open, like the kind of person you would want to meet yourself.
- It's always worth getting a friend (or friends) to comment on your profile. They will tell you if you are being too modest, too arrogant, or just sound plain crazy.
- There are professional profile writing services available and some sites even have a coach or customer care team that can assist you. Use them if you do not feel confident about your writing skills.
- Don't put off writing a profile or skip questions on the way through. It gives a signal that you are not taking the process seriously, and could mean potential matches write you off immediately.

Next, you will be invited to upload your photograph. Don't worry if you're not especially computer literate. The dating sites will make it easy for you.

You are nine times more likely to get approaches online if you include a photograph.

Choose a picture in which you are smiling and looking at the camera, with your eyes wide open. This will make potential matches feel as though you are looking at them. Don't choose a picture that is a decade old or your date will be in for a shock when they first meet you. It probably doesn't need to be said, but avoid silly costumes, revealing outfits, making funny faces, or wearing sunglasses. Just be sure to look your natural best.

Some sites allow you to upload secondary photos, and you can use these to illustrate your passions. Post that picture of you singing your lungs out at a Bruce Springsteen concert, or climbing Kilimanjaro, or riding an elephant in Kerala. Once you have finished the registration process, you're all set to go. On a photo site, just start hunting through the pictures of people in your location. On a matchmaking site, they will send you your potential matches for consideration. You can then wait for someone to make contact with you—or, if you are absorbing the message of this book, you will take control yourself.

PHOTO QUALITY

Web cams and mobile phones might seem convenient, but the photos are often grainy. It's better to get hold of a good digital camera or use a traditional film camera and scan the photos in high resolution. Choose a soft, flattering light source and position yourself off to one side of it. Broad daylight can be unflattering, but sitting or standing near a window indoors can work well. Don't pose in front of a busy background; the background should be muted so that your face is the main focus of the picture. Keep your chin up so that it doesn't look as though you have a double chin. If you find it hard to look directly at the camera without blinking, look off to one side, ask the photographer to tell you when they are ready, and look forward at the last minute. This gives a natural look, as opposed to a deer-in-the-headlights stare.

Making approaches online

Old-fashioned wisdom says that men should be the ones to make the first move. They are the hunters and their macho pride can be wounded by pushy women. Well, scratch that. We're not living in caves these days. That rusty scenario is no longer current, and men are totally receptive to approaches from women online—in fact, according to surveys, they feel flattered by and receptive to women who make the first move. If you like someone and want to meet them, it doesn't matter whether you are male or female—go ahead and make the first move. Send a friendly icebreaker "nudge" or email. Waiting around for something to happen makes it far less likely to happen than if you take action. You are always better off controlling your own fate.

When trying to spark someone's interest by email, you've got to be fun, engaging, and good at creating a rapport, while still retaining an element of mystery. The same advice applies as when you are creating your profile, although you should ask thought-provoking questions about the other person as well—but not in a Spanish Inquisition type of way. Keep it light.

Make your emails concise, using two-to-three sentence replies. No one wants to trawl through your entire life story. If in doubt, draft an email, walk away, and return an hour later to review it, edit it, and, when satisfied, press send. One survey of eHarmony users listed the following grievances when it comes to emailing:

- Poor spelling and grammar.
- The use of text speak, such as "How r u? gr8 to spk to u."
- A generic message that has obviously been sent to lots of people, such as "Hi, wanna chat?" It implies that the other person couldn't even be bothered to read your profile and take an interest in you personally.
- Going on about yourself at length, without asking any questions about the other person.
- Ignoring questions you asked in your previous email.
- Short, uninformative answers to questions—"Had a good week, work busy"—don't help you get to know the other person.

Be completely honest about yourself, so that you attract matches who will respect you, warts and all. Expect the same in return. If you catch someone in a lie, call them on it or break off contact. If it's a lie that could have detrimental effects for anyone else (for example, if they are married but pretending to be single), report them to the agency concerned, and move on quickly.

You'll know whether there is a connection after a few emails back and forth. If you're not interested, make it tactfully clear as soon as possible. Never lead someone on. If a match contacts you and you're not interested, be respectful enough to send a short and thoughtful rejection, explaining your reasons, but not in a cruel way. Maybe they live too far away, or you don't want to get involved with someone who has children. In those cases, just say so politely.

Karen and John

Karen started dating again a month or two after splitting up from an eleven-year relationship. She dated men she met through mutual friends, a couple of men she met in day-to-day life, and some she met at singles' events. She dated a lot and had a very clear idea of what kind of relationship she was looking for, but no one matched up. She started looking at online dating sites with some girlfriends and they all had a good laugh, although they came across a lot of men who she says were obviously playing games. But when she came across eHarmony, the initial questionnaire was so detailed she knew right away that she was onto something that would attract a better caliber of person. The guys sounded much more genuine than on other sites, and after corresponding with a few, she got in touch with John. He lived in Denver, Colorado, and she lived in Windsor, England, but the day after their first phone conversation he flew across the Atlantic to come to a housewarming party she was throwing. And that was the start of a relationship that has now resulted in them having a fairy-tale wedding and a happy lifestyle that still includes lots of transatlantic flights!

MULTI-DATING

The savviest singles know that dating is a numbers game. Instead of putting all their emotional eggs in one basket, they will date several people at one time. The benefits of this are that they don't feel so much pressure to make one specific date work because there are plenty more out there. However, it means that you need to be aware when you call or meet someone that they may have several potential matches in differing stages of communication. Relationships online don't become exclusive until you mutually agree that they are and take your profiles down from the site.

The first call

A potential pitfall of dating online is that people can get lulled into a passive email exchange that lasts for months, rather than an actual date. The danger of this is that you can become emotionally invested in a potential match, only to discover that when you meet in person, the spark isn't there.

When you start sharing personal information with someone, it's easy to feel as though you have made a deep connection right away. You may be emailing each other a few times a day, looking forward to your match's replies, but never assume that this means you will have the same connection in person. They may not talk how they write, and the chemistry might not be there. Besides, if you communicate by email for months before speaking on the phone, you'll put a lot of pressure on the call, so it's best to initiate a call sooner rather than later.

Go at your own pace, of course, and don't let yourself be pressured into making that initial call or arranging a first date before you are ready. But don't forget that no matter how you meet someone, there will always be a little nervousness. Try to balance feeling comfortable with an awareness that there are always going to be nerves.

You'll probably be less nervous if you phone as soon as a connection is clear, rather than several months down the line.

Yet again, if a woman sits at home waiting for the man to call, she could significantly reduce her chances of ever meeting her match. If you are interested, take the plunge and do it. Take a deep breath and dial the number, remembering that you don't have the monopoly on nerves—the other person is likely to be on edge as well.

Keep the conversation brief. Don't pin all your hopes on a first call. If you are proactive on an online dating site, you are likely to have phone conversations with numerous matches.

A call isn't necessarily a request for a get-together. It's about hearing your match's voice and laugh and getting a sense of who they are.

If the call goes well, you may decide you'd like to meet up. Nothing ventured, nothing gained. There's advice on how to approach first dates in chapter six, but the basics are: choose a public place for the first couple of dates, and limit the time so you're not stuck there for hours and hours. Lunch or an afternoon coffee are much better ideas than a night out in a bar. You might be tempted to have an alcoholic drink to take the edge off your nerves, but it will mean your instincts are not as sharp as they could be, so it's not advisable for a first date.

Keeping safe

There is always an element of risk when you start getting to know a stranger and giving them information about yourself. Second-time-around daters have more life experience and should be better able to pick out the rotten apples from the fruit bowl than novices. If someone arouses your suspicions, don't hang around—make a quick exit.

One of the advantages of dating sites is that they erect a firewall between you and potential matches. You don't put your home number, your email address, or any other personal details online. No one will find out where you live unless you tell them. When you reply to emails, you send them anonymously through the agency. Most dating agencies also offer a service whereby you can call and talk to each other without revealing your phone numbers. Take advantage of these services until you have met the other person and are sure you feel comfortable with them. When you do, follow the advice on first dates in chapter six, such as meeting in a public place, telling someone where you will be, and checking in with them during the date.

It's sad, but true, that there are a small number of fraudsters out there. Online agencies do their best to keep their user pools free of people who are not seriously looking for a partner, but the odd one might slip in. For example, you may find a very charming match who seems genuine but lives far away and needs money for the airfare to meet you. Under no circumstances should you give money to anyone you haven't met and really gotten to know. Additionally, there are a few serial seducers who think they will find a ready supply of sexual partners via online dating sites, but if enough people report them to the agency, they will be struck off the books. Remember at all times to take things at your own pace, and never allow yourself to be pushed into moving faster than you feel comfortable with.

As in the world at large, there are bad people online, so be as cautious as you would be if you met a stranger in the supermarket, the Laundromat, or at a sports event. You wouldn't invite them into your home or lend them money until you had spent enough time with them to feel sure they were good people. Apply the same basic common sense to anyone you meet via the Internet.

You have more protection if you meet someone through a dating agency than if you meet them in the course of your daily life, because you can take your time to find out more about them, keep your personal details secure, and complain to the agency about bad behavior—and your date knows this.

Look for signs of inconsistency. If their emails contradict something they've said in their profile, or if you meet them and they seem like a completely different person in the flesh from how they did on the phone, it may signal that they haven't been genuine and you should end communication. Be aware that people can sound strange when they're nervous, but don't stifle your instincts. If your gut tells you something is not right, then it probably isn't.

If someone you have met through an online agency becomes abusive or creepy, you should contact the agency and report it. They will have a complaints procedure in place and certain levels of action they can take against the abuser. However, if someone starts stalking you or threatens you and makes you genuinely scared, don't hesitate to report them to the police.

Whenever someone sets off your internal alarm bells, pay attention and act accordingly, no matter how you met them. This applies just as much if mutual friends introduced you as if you got in touch online. Don't ever take risks with your personal safety.

Dealing with rejection

Rejection after one or two meetings is something you should take in your stride in the modern world. Think of dating as a gourmet-food-tasting event with thousands of different delicacies to try. Some may be too sweet for you, some too bitter; you may not like the texture of one, or the appearance of another. It doesn't mean they are bad foods; it's all about personal taste. The great thing is there are plenty more foods out there, so if you keep trying you will find the perfect one eventually, and someone is bound to fall for the "taste" of you as well.

It's much easier to deal with rejection when dating online than it would be with someone you met at a friend's party.

- If you send an icebreaker email to someone online and they don't reply, it's because some detail of your description doesn't match their shopping list. However, if you meet someone at a party and approach them for a conversation but they take the first opportunity to move away, it's probably because they aren't attracted to you.
- Exchanging emails constitutes little more than virtual flirting. There is no real relationship, they don't know the real you, so if your match stops communicating, there's no reason to take it to heart.
- When you meet someone you've been communicating with online, it's like a blind date. If they decide they don't want a second date, it probably just means that for them, the chemistry is not there. There's nothing you can do about that short of having a DNA transplant, so get over it.

However, if you find you are getting a string of rejections without any positive results, look at the stage at which it is happening.

- People not responding to your icebreaker emails? Ask a friend to look at your profile and judge whether there is anything off-putting in there, and make sure you are approaching people with whom you are checking all the compatibility boxes.
- Is communication coming to an abrupt halt after a few emails? Could it be that you are coming on too strong or sounding weird in some way? Swallow your pride and ask for feedback from one or two people who have faded out on you.

- If you are not getting a second date, read the advice in chapter six and try to work out if you are making any basic errors. Once again, you could ask your date for feedback.

No matter what method you are using to meet potential partners, the key is to keep trying and bring the same fresh enthusiasm to each new encounter, because they just could be The One. It's only natural to feel downhearted after a few awkward dates and a couple of rejections, but remember that the more people you date, the faster you will find the relationship you are looking for. Keep putting yourself out there in the field, be proactive, and be honest with yourself and the people you meet, and it will happen for you in time.

If you feel you are getting jaded after a string of bad dates or rejections and your energy and enthusiasm are running low, take a couple of months off. You might be surprised to find that the moment you stop looking is the moment when the right person suddenly appears! Ask people how they met their partners and you'll often hear some variation on this: "I wasn't planning to go to that party because I was fed up with the singles scene, but I changed my mind at the last minute and... " The minute they stop trying is the minute when it happens. We can't guarantee it will work this way for you but if you are fed up, it's certainly worth a go. In chapter six, you'll find advice on how to approach a first date so as to give you and your potential partner a chance to get to know each other a bit more and pick up some further clues about whether they could be the right person for you.

Katy and Stu

Katy was a single parent to an eight-month-old daughter and had been single since finding herself pregnant. She found herself sitting in the house alone most nights with little to do, and she decided to look at dating websites, just out of curiosity. At first, she didn't intend to sign up, but there were some nice-looking men so she paid for a month's trial. After filling in her details initially she didn't get many matches, so she took away a few of her strict preferences and kept looking.

About seven days into her search she came across Stu. His profile didn't give much away, but he looked like her type: tall, rugged, a fireman, liked nights in, and wanted marriage and babies eventually. They emailed for a while and she began to like him more and more, but she was worried that he might not like her in the flesh when they eventually met up. She hadn't been on a date in three years and was petrified, but she needn't have been. Soon after meeting, Stu said: "I know we agreed to not get ahead of ourselves until we've had a date and got to know each other better, but I think you're lovely, and I already know I'd like to see you again."

Their second date was New Year's Eve, and on the third date he met and started to fall in love with Katy's little daughter. They are now getting married, and Katy is still dazzled by what has happened to her. She joined the dating site for a bit of fun, perhaps a bit of flirting practice to get her ready for the dating world, and, instead, she found a new husband and a new father for her baby girl.

CHAPTER SIX

Do's and Don'ts
on the First Date

You've arranged where to meet, you've decided what to wear (casual but stylish), and you know how to get there. This can often be when the nerves hit. What if I make a complete idiot of myself by spilling a drink over my date, or by tripping over my own feet? What if I can't think of anything to say? And then the big one: What if I like them and they don't like me?

Some children are afraid of dogs, and the fear makes them act strangely, hiding behind their parent or making scared noises. Dogs sense the weirdness and may bark at them instead of wagging their tails in greeting. The more they bark, the more terrified the child becomes. As adults, most of us have learned how dogs behave so we're comfortable around them, even if we've never met that particular one before—and they reward us by getting over their guard dog mentality and being friendly.

The same scenario applies to dating. If you think your nervousness about dating tends to make you act a little weird and scares off your dates, here are some ideas to put you more at your ease. The key to it all is planning, preparation, and control. If you choose the right kind of place to meet, and have everything ready that you will need, then you will feel more in control—and more relaxed.

- Arrange to meet in a place you are familiar with, on your home territory. If you know somewhere with a good atmosphere and great coffee, you've got fewer things to worry about. Make sure it's not too expensive, though; your date may expect to pay their half of the tab and be embarrassed if they can't afford it.
- A date involving an activity, such as cycling around a pretty lake, or a trip to a museum, can help to calm the nerves by giving you something to focus on. But avoid anything too interest-specific, such as an evening of 17th century Persian poetry.
- Also avoid very noisy places, or events that can attract a raucous crowd, such as loud sporting events or rock concerts. Your date should feel safe—and you should be able to communicate without resorting to sign language.
- Choose an activity that can be cut short gracefully if it's not working. If you take your date to a baseball game, you could be stuck with them through the whole nine innings.
- It goes without saying, but don't invite someone to meet you at your home on a first date. Choose somewhere safe and public.
- Make sure you have enough cash to cover the cost of your coffee and a cab ride home in an emergency. Think about the image you wish to project and what you plan to wear in plenty of time. Choose something you feel confident wearing, and add a quick splash of your favorite aftershave or perfume.
- Prepare some topics of conversation to fill any awkward pauses. Try to choose subjects you know the other person is interested in, or memorize a couple of particularly funny anecdotes. There are some suggestions for conversation openers on page 117.
- Remember that one date is not a big deal. Don't put too much pressure on yourself. If you treat an outing with another human being as sudden-death overtime for your entire future, you're going to be giving off some very scary vibes.
- Realize that your date could be feeling exactly the same way as you are; perhaps, they're even more nervous. Relax and remember that you are just forming an opinion of each other. You're not standing up to perform a solo in Carnegie Hall.

You might not eliminate your nervousness entirely, but try to reduce it to a fraction of what it could be, a mere symptom rather than a full-blown syndrome. Know and understand that there's a lot less riding on an individual date than the butterflies in your stomach might be telling you.

Carron and Graham

Graham knew he liked the look of Carron when he saw her standing at the bar at a friend's party, but he was so nervous when he approached her that he said something completely idiotic: "That's a hideous hat you're wearing." She was taken aback and mumbled, "Gosh, I suppose I should have taken it off since we're indoors, but my hair is a mess." They could have gone their separate ways at that moment, but, fortunately, Graham was able to find something more friendly to say, they started a conversation, and before Carron left, he had asked her out on a date the following week. They met in a restaurant, had a meal, then went on to a late-night bar where they sat in a dimly lit booth. Graham managed to drop his wallet on the floor, Carron bent down to help him find it, he straightened up, not realizing she was there—and his elbow connected with her cheek. Hard. She didn't want to make a huge fuss but her face was really hurting, so finally she said she thought she had better go to the ER. Graham went with her, full of shame, and convinced that the hospital staff would think he had hit her deliberately. They took an X-ray and it transpired that she had a hairline fracture of the cheekbone. Is it possible for a date to go any worse than this? Surely not. You'd think that would have been the end of things—but, in fact, they got married and have been together for twenty years now.

MAKE YOUR FIRST DATE SAFE

Do:
- Meet in a public place, at a decent hour.
- Make your own way there. It's not a good idea to get into a stranger's car.
- Tell someone where and when you're going, and if possible "check in" with them at some point.
- Make sure your mobile is fully charged and you have the numbers you need.

Don't:
- Drink too much. It's safest not to drink alcohol at all.
- Leave your drink or any personal belongings with your date if you step away for any reason.
- Meet at your home or workplace.

Being a good date

The most important thing on a date is to be genuinely interested in who the other person is. Listen to the stories they tell you, ask questions about their life, and be as natural as you can be. Imagine you're out with a friend of a friend whom you are trying to get to know, because they've just moved to town and are going to enter your social circle. You wouldn't dive in with a laundry list of questions, forcing them to jump from topic to topic. Age? Check. Career plans? Check. Nice car? Check. A conversation should flow, with one subject leading on from the next. On pages 115–121 you will find a list of first-date "don'ts," and if you do the opposite from all of them you'll be well on the way to having a good date!

One study has uncovered that men are particularly attracted to women who laugh at their jokes. Women don't care quite so much whether they can make men laugh, but it's still appreciated. On a date, a laugh at the right moment can show not only that you're listening, but also that what they're saying is funny. This conveys aptitude in your ability to understand a joke and similarity in your senses of humor, which is a positive sign of compatibility.

Laughing also affects your physiology. It decreases blood pressure, while increasing oxygenation of the blood and the flow of blood to your skin, thus making you look healthier. Laughter can decrease stress levels and raise your feelings of excitement and joy, stimulating reward areas of the brain.

> *As you laugh together, you create social bonds, inside jokes, and overall positive experiences.*

Make sure you are laughing together, though. Be observant of the other person's reactions and check that they're not just pinning a polite smile on their face while you roll in the aisles at your own jokes. Watching the other person's body language (see page 112–115) will give you clues about how they're feeling throughout the date. Respond to these clues and you will automatically feel more in tune with each other.

Consideration for your date will go a long way toward showing them that you are a decent person. If their drink is running low, call the waiter and have it refilled. Ask if they're hungry and want something to eat. Don't fuss over them, but offer common courtesy. Try very hard not to spill your drink down the front of them, but if the worst comes to the worst, grab some towels to help clean it up, apologize, and offer to pay for the dry cleaning.

On a first date, it's best to have a prearranged time at which you go your separate ways. An hour or two is enough for a first meeting, and if you have agreed on this in advance you will both know where you stand. Make sure you have organized your own transportation so you don't have to rely on your date to give you a lift home.

WHO PAYS?

On a first date, when you don't yet know if you will be having a second, it is fairest to split the check. If a date insists on treating you, you could feel badly if you decide you don't want to see them again. However, you may find that people with more traditional attitudes still expect the man to pay. If it's just a coffee and a muffin, that's fine, but if it is a three-course dinner with expensive wine, not so much. Letting a man pick up the check time after time introduces a dynamic into the relationship that he is the one in charge, and in the 21st century fewer people feel comfortable slotting into such old-fashioned roles.

When the date comes to a close, thank the other person and offer them a quick handshake or hug (whatever feels right). Wondering how you can tell if a goodbye kiss is in the cards? Chances are good that your date will give you some kind of verbal or physical clues toward the end of your encounter. For example, if they step closer when saying goodbye, lean in during your parting conversation, tell you that it was a great date, or linger during your goodbye hug, these are all signs that they might want you to make the next move. If you pick up any signal, proceed according to your own comfort level. For example, if you're interested and ready, go ahead and lean in for a gentle goodnight kiss. Most likely, your date will respond by kissing you back. If you have read the signals wrong, they will pull away.

> *Don't pounce on your date; a first kiss should be brief. There will be plenty of time for more passionate kissing if you continue dating.*

When appropriate, let your date know if you'd like to go out again. If they feel the same, they will respond favorably. At that point, tell your date when and how you'll be in contact with them—and keep your word. If you are not interested, be honest, but let them down easy. Tell them that you think they are a great person but that the chemistry is not there for you, or explain that you are dating several other people and may have met someone else you're interested in. Stick close to the truth without being mean. Treat someone as you would like to be treated! Don't ever tell anyone that you'll call or that you'd like to make another date without meaning it. Leaving someone dangling emotionally will cause confusion on their part, and you know you wouldn't like it if it happened to you.

Keep any final exchange brief, thus avoiding the awkwardness of a lingering/stammering/downward spiral at the end of a date. The whole date should be relaxed and fun, creating the ideal environment for you to be yourself and allowing your date the space and comfort to do the same.

When you get home, write some notes in your dating notebook about how you think the date went, and think about anything you might do differently next time. Dating is a learning process, so make sure you pick up the lessons and you'll be all set to impress when the person you want to be a big hit with comes along.

Reading body language
Much of face-to-face communication is in body language and tone of voice. How people act, and how they sound, is more important than what they say, so you will be missing out on some vital dating clues if you don't tune in to the body language of others.

Someone's body language can be very subtle and easy to misinterpret, however, so keep in mind that individual cues are not all-or-nothing observations. Even if you notice a few indicators of flagging interest, it doesn't mean you don't still have a chance. It is the sum of all body language cues that will clue you in to how well you're hitting it off.

There are two general categories of body language that can help you assess whether someone shares your same interest level: open and closed.

Open body language usually indicates that a person is interested in you or is receptive to your advances. Generally, a person who is expressing open body language is relaxed in stance, with arms and legs uncrossed, and they may use their hands to animate their conversation. Also look for the following open body language cues:

- Eye-to-eye contact between two interested people is held for longer than usual (although too much eye contact can be off-putting, as if the other person wants to dominate you).
- Preening gestures, such as someone running fingers through their own hair and tossing the head slightly to the side, are a sign of interest. They might fiddle with jewelry, cufflinks, or their watch.
- Leaning inward or closer toward a person to gauge a response means they don't want to miss anything.
- Subtle head nods while the other person is talking show they're engaged.
- Touching the other person on the arm, hand, or shoulder when making a point in conversation can be conscious or subconscious flirtation.
- Licking or biting the lips is a sign of desire. Most signs of desire are centered on the lips.
- Some people will position themselves between the object of interest and any other potential suitors in the environment.
- Genuine smiles that reach the eyes are always a good sign.

Closed body language usually indicates that a person is expressing some lack of interest or apprehension in getting to know you further. They may appear tense or defensive in the shoulders, with arms either crossed or tucked upward behind the head with the elbows facing outward. Also look for these other common closed body language cues:

- A person may avoid eye contact altogether, as if to hide their true feelings about you. They might look around the room, feigning interest in other people or objects to avoid your gaze.
- Like looking away, staying perfectly still can sometimes help a person hide negative feelings toward someone else.
- Curling the shoulders inward slightly and pointing the chin downward are defensive gestures.
- Leaning away from or physically moving away from the other person, even subtly, can indicate a subconscious desire to get away.

MIRRORING

If your date adopts the same position as you, crossing their legs at the same time or picking up a drink when you do, it could be that they are feeling in tune with you—or it might be that they know about the theory of mirroring and *want* to be in tune with you. We like people who are similar to us, and by sitting and moving in the same way as another person, we give out a subconscious signal that we are trustworthy, like them, so it's a good way of creating rapport. Don't overdo it though, or your date will think you are mocking them.

Mixed messages

Someone may seem to like you from the way they are talking, yet their body language is closed. Or they might lean in toward you but avoid eye contact. Such mixed messages are difficult to interpret, because there are several possible explanations.

- The person is not interested in you, but is deceiving you by pretending to like you so as not to be rude.
- The person may be interested in you, perhaps even a great deal, but they're nervous and are not sure how you feel about them. Anxious or shy people can come across as aloof and uninterested when they're anything but.

- There could be external conditions you may not be aware of. Maybe their ex has just walked into the restaurant, or perhaps they have a bad back and are trying to get comfortable. Sometimes a person might cross their arms because they are feeling slightly chilly, yet you perceive it as being defensive.

Put all your instincts and impressions of both spoken and unspoken communication together to make your best judgment about how well you're hitting it off with someone you're interested in. Then use your judgment to lead your behavior on the date. It's alright to be one step ahead of the other person—someone has to make the first moves—but if they are glancing at their watch and seeming anxious to leave, it's not a good time to lurch in for a passionate kiss or ask them if they want to meet up again.

What not to do on a first date

The following list may seem long, but most points are glaringly obvious. The problem is that we're not always aware of the way we are coming across. Few people are rude enough to stand up and say: "You're insane. I'm leaving." They'll sit quietly, nod, and wait for a chance to yawn discreetly, then announce: "Wow, is that the time? I've got to get up early tomorrow." And we all know what that means.

If you are coming back to dating after a long time away, you may need to work on your dating skills, and this means some self-reflection. It might not be easy, but it will make you a better prospect.

There are a few general things to remember that will make a first date easier. A first date is about getting to know each other. You have to reveal things about yourself, and you should learn things about your partner, so ask questions, but don't forget to reciprocate their disclosures with your own. If one person is dominating the conversation on the date, it probably isn't going well.

People like those who disclose information about themselves and who reciprocate by asking questions and responding to the answers.

If you find that people don't tend to want to see you again after a first date, read through the following types of behavior (in recent research all of these were turn-offs) and do some honest soul-searching to see if you might be guilty of any of them.

Monopolizing the conversation

Sometimes we are so invested in "selling" ourselves that we go on and on in our attempt to let our date know how great we are. Chatting about how wild you were back in your college days, or about all the great parties you've been to, is not very exciting for a date to listen to. The detailed minutiae of your job will only be interesting to someone else in the same field (and maybe not even then). Even tales of exotic travels can drag on a bit. Keep your anecdotes short, even if you think they are the most fascinating stories you've ever heard. Don't go on about a great time you had at some point in the past that your date wasn't part of. It gives the impression that your current life is somehow less interesting.

Rather than selling themselves, some people display their insecurities by apologizing for their shortcomings, or complaining about their jobs, family, and friends. (See "Over-sharing," opposite.) Sometimes we just get nervous and rush to fill awkward gaps with "chatter."

Whatever the reason that tempts you to monopolize the conversation, resist it. Try to focus on the moment at hand and be fully present for the other person. Test whether you have done this after the date, by giving the person an entry in your dating notebook and jotting down key facts you learned about them during the date that you didn't know already. Can't think of many? That probably means you were doing all the talking...

CONVERSATIONAL OPENERS

Why not plan a few open-ended questions to ask your date. Some ideas could be:

- Describe your perfect Sunday. Where would you go, what would you do?
- Do you have any pets? If you were getting a pet, what kind would you get?
- Try a "would you rather?" conversation. For example, would you rather give up your mobile phone or your car?
- If you got a windfall of cash what would you do with it?
- What is the most foolish thing you've ever done in your life? Be prepared to share your own stories of that tattoo you now regret, or the time you lost your passport on the luggage carousel at Miami airport.

Over-sharing

Self disclosure and openness are key to deepening the connection between two people, but there is such a thing as offering too much information when you've only just met. It can be a major turn-off if someone immediately begins opening up about their fear of losing their job, their father's heart condition, or their psychological and emotional problems. Telling your date about your scheduled ingrown toenail operation is not sexy, and they really don't want to know that you have irritable bowel syndrome and try to avoid wheat.

Into this category comes talking about past partners. If the anecdote is negative, you'll come off looking like a bitter victim; if it's positive, you'll seem as though you're still pining for them. If you talk about a fabulous trip you and your ex took together, it could make your date feel inadequate, wondering whether they can afford to take such trips with you. If they ask about your previous partner, it's fine to give the basic facts: "We were together for a year but she got offered a

job on the other side of the country and my work kept me here."
Don't dis your ex, though.

Bragging

Boasting about famous people you've met, or how much your new house cost, or how wonderful your boss thinks you are, are all no-nos. Imagine how you would feel if you were on the receiving end of any of the following conversational non-starters.

"I just bought this incredible new BMW. I'd been thinking about getting a sports car for years, then I got a nice bonus and decided to take the plunge."

There isn't much to say, unless you happen to be a German car fanatic.

"I got a backstage pass after the concert and we were just standing around when Eric Clapton actually passed me in the hall."

Even a diehard Clapton fan would struggle to find this impressive.

"My boss has given me sole responsibility for getting clearance forms signed by the compliance people, which means he must really trust me."

Surely there are more interesting aspects of your job?

The problem is that people have no idea they are coming across in this way. They think they are dazzling you with their fabulous lifestyle and achievements instead of boring the pants off you. Be warned, and remember to listen to yourself and censor any tendency you might have to boast (or bore). Your date's body language may be giving you clues if you care to pick up on them. The trick is to try and find connections between you and the other person, and that involves listening and responding rather than delivering monologues.

Coming on too strong

First dates should be light and fun, rather than a job interview to assess a potential future husband or wife. While it may be your ultimate goal is to find a soul mate and/or someone to have children with, save that conversation for several months down the line. Even a man who is open to the idea of settling down might be scared off by a woman who mentions her ticking biological clock within the first half hour, and women can be put off by men who ask on the first date: "When are you thinking of having children?" It makes you sound intense and desperate and indeed some women may have already had them. Lighten up!

The key is to focus on being fully present during your time with your date, and save tomorrow for tomorrow.

> *Before you drag them to a clinic for a blood test to check whether they have any genetic disorders they could pass on to your offspring, try to find out whether you actually enjoy each other's company.*

In the same vein, the first date is way too soon to tell someone that you think they could be "The One," or that you can imagine yourself falling in love with them. People who fall in love too quickly are falling in love with an ideal rather than a reality. There's more about this on page 128. Most of us take longer than a nanosecond to realize we've found true love. If you've fast-tracked the process, keep quiet about your feelings until sure the other person has caught up with you.

Talking about sex

Asking someone about their sexual preferences on a first date is way too forward. A person's sexual needs and desires are deeply intimate; come across as too brash, and they may never share them with you. You'll appear somewhat pervy if you ask intrusive questions, and they'll get the impression that you are only interested in a sexual relationship.

Pushing your agenda

Banging the drum about your politics or trying to convert someone to your religion are both off-putting on a date. The fact is that even if you are compatible in these areas, using your date time to harangue the other person with your beliefs can make you seem obsessive. On first dates, most of us are looking for signs that might warn us off a person who is going to be trouble down the line, and this one is a flashing neon sign in the sky.

Talking about other people you're dating

In this day and age, it is quite acceptable to date several people at the same time, so long as everyone knows the situation. Multi-dating is especially common if you meet online. But the last thing you want to hear on a date are details about other dating encounters. You might want to talk about the process of online dating, and there's nothing wrong with that, but you don't want to hear how many dates the other person has been on that haven't worked out, or the fact that no one else has agreed to a date with them in the two years they've been signed up!

Getting drunk

If you're nervous, it might be tempting to loosen up by having a quick drink before you meet your date. They then ask if you would like a beer or a glass of wine and they're having one as well, and then another, and before you know it, you are drunk. From now on, your instincts are going to be very blurry, so you won't be able to make clear judgments about the other person, or about yourself. People who have too much to drink tend to think they are being fabulously witty and clever as they slur their words and repeat themselves. You could argue that if you are both drunk it doesn't matter, but peering at someone through "beer goggles" is hardly a great way to get to know them. And they might not be quite as drunk as you.

Borrowing money from your date

Not bringing enough money with you to pay for your share of the date implies that you are either broke, a freeloader, or hopelessly unorganized. And asking to borrow money to make your overdue rent payment is a sign that you are incapable of looking after yourself. Even billionaires will think twice about dating spongers.

Dealing with bad dates

You arrive and know at first glance that it's not going to work for you. There's no chemistry, they're wearing an appalling shirt, and they look twenty years older than they did in their photograph. You may feel like turning and walking right out the door, but it's common courtesy to sit down, have a quick coffee, and listen to whatever they have to say for themselves. Remember: first impressions can be wildly inaccurate.

If, after the obligatory conversation, you are still convinced you are wasting your time, it's fine to say so. Be polite about it, wish them luck, thank them for meeting you, and move along. Even if the conversation lacked spark, you never know if this meeting might prove beneficial in the future. Perhaps you have learned something new, garnered a new business contact, or just practiced a little patience. Don't make enemies: you never know whether they'll turn up in future as new clients of your business or as the fiancé of one of your best friends.

If you're dating online and you've had a string of bad dates, it's easy to get disheartened. Re-examine the criteria you are using to select the people you date, and get an honest opinion from a friend about the impression your profile gives, and then rewrite it if necessary. Sometimes it's a good idea to take a few months off from dating if you feel your enthusiasm is waning. When you come back, there should be lots of new matches to choose from and your energy and optimism should return.

Jeremy and Linda

Jeremy had broken up with a long-term girlfriend, quit his job, and was looking for something different, so he joined eHarmony. He was really nervous before his first date and things got worse after she arrived and clearly didn't like what she saw. She downed half a drink, made a transparent excuse, and left. It could have been a soul-destroying experience, but fortunately he already had five more dates lined up. Date number two was fun, but it was obvious it wasn't going to work for either of them. They had dinner as friends, then went their separate ways. Dates three and four weren't memorable. Date five was good and he'd made an arrangement to see her again when along came date six—Linda! They met for a drink, hit it off so well it became dinner, and he knew things looked good when she sent him a nice text on the way home. He let date five down gently, and the rest, as they say, is history. Jeremy and Linda are now married and expecting their first child.

Reading through this chapter, you may have chuckled, recognizing some of the types of behavior from the dates that you've had in the past. You may have cringed, remembering times when you perhaps had one drink too many and bored your date to tears with tales of your college exploits, or the time you were voted "coolest dancer" at your high school graduation. But we want you to leave this chapter thinking positively. The vast majority of people looking for relationships are nice, vulnerable, trustworthy souls, just like you. When you arrange a date, you have the chance to dip your toe in the water and make a brief connection with another person that may or may not lead to something more. Nothing ventured, nothing gained. There's someone out there for everyone, and you might find the person for you on your very next date. So what are you waiting for?

A FIRST-DATE CHECKLIST

- Meet in a safe place, during the daytime if you can.
- Arrange your own transportation to and from the date.
- Choose a short meeting—a couple of hours at most.
- Smile and make eye contact.
- Be friendly and interested in the other person.
- Answer their questions openly, and try to keep it fun.
- Watch their body language and respond accordingly.
- Split the check, unless otherwise agreed beforehand.
- Say a polite goodbye and thank the other person for the date.

CHAPTER SEVEN

The Early Weeks

During the first weeks and months of dating, you'll be learning more about each other all the time. Everything is a first: the first time you have dinner together, first date at the movies, first time you invite them to your home, and first time you see theirs as well.

You'll learn factual stuff—that they have an orange sofa, a Picasso print, and a cat named Henry. But much more important will be the lessons you are learning about their core values and vital attributes. This is your best chance to decide how well their qualities match yours, as well as checking whether they meet your "must have" and "can't stand" criteria. You want to do this before making too much of an emotional investment in the relationship so you can have an easier time walking away, if necessary.

It's not advisable to sit the potential partner down with your dating notebook open on your knee and subject them to a lengthy questionnaire. Get to know the person, be genuinely interested in who they are, and the insights you need will emerge naturally as part of the ongoing conversation. Don't try to impose an artificial timeline—"We must be exclusive once we've been dating for a month"; "She should say she loves me after three months"; "He must have asked me to marry him when we've been together for eighteen months." Says who? Timelines place constraints on a relationship and stop it from evolving naturally.

Before you start worrying about the next step, try to find out whether this is the right person for you to be with, or whether you need to find someone else.

You're not going to learn everything you need to know on day one. The great thing about dating is that you can have lots of fun along the way while you're thinking in the back of your mind: "Are they fulfilling the things that I really need in a relationship?"

In this chapter, we will go over some basic guidelines about those first few weeks of getting to know someone. The excitement of starting a new relationship can be overwhelming. Finding someone you connect with, and are attracted to, may have your head spinning with all the possibilities of what the relationship could become. But the rush of emotion can also be blinding, keeping you from seeing the incompatibilities and danger signs that will eventually spell trouble for the relationship later on. You need to keep in mind all of the factors that you know are important in making a relationship work. Here is where all of your experience can be valuable in finding the right person.

One thing to keep in mind is that the suggestions in this chapter are just guidelines. There are no hard and fast rules that dictate when something is right or wrong, because every relationship is different. Some rare couples (well, very rare couples) know right off the bat that they are right for each other and live happily ever after. For the rest of us, it takes some time to make sure we've found the right person. It could be a few months; it might even be a couple of years. Maybe one partner will want to move faster than the other, especially if there is a big reason—such as a biological clock—to move things along. Just don't rush so fast that you find yourself with a ring on your finger looking over the breakfast table at someone you don't truly know and love.

THE BIOLOGICAL CLOCK DILEMMA

If you are a thirty-five-year-old woman who wants to have children, you need to know sooner rather than later if your boyfriend wants the same thing. But to ask him directly could scare him off. The subject of kids might come up naturally at some point in the early weeks, but if it doesn't, there are plenty of other ways to figure out whether he is looking to settle down. Assess his lifestyle. Does he have a steady job? Has he been in the area for some time, or does he have a metaphorical backpack on? People who are at the stage of thinking about creating a family have usually been living in one place for some time and seem fairly settled. If he comes from a big family, ask him how he liked it. The more seamlessly you can allow information simply to emerge as part of your normal conversation, the less pressure your partner will feel. Wait until you can sense that things are getting more serious for both of you before pressing him further, or he could feel as if all you are looking for is a father for your children.

Are they right for you?

As people get older, they tend to have a clearer picture of themselves. Personality becomes more crystallized and it is less likely to change. If you meet someone at fifteen, you're likely to be quite different by the time you're twenty. But if you meet someone at forty-five, you're probably not going to be that much different by fifty-five. This means there's less room to grow toward each other in a second-time-around relationship, which places a bigger premium on making sure you're compatible from the outset. Below are reminders of some of the issues to watch out for so you can be sure you're on the right path.

Are you falling into an old, unhealthy pattern?

Everyone has blind spots. Being treated in an unacceptable way may start small and grow before you notice, or you may be overwhelmed by attraction and infatuation and ignore important warning signs of what is to come. Here are some types of behavior that may signal that something is wrong. They don't necessarily mean that the relationship is doomed, or that partner is a bad egg, but you should pay attention because there may be bigger problems lurking.

- On a date, do you always pick up the check because your partner is unable to pay for some reason?
- Does your partner criticize you a lot?
- Does your partner try to control aspects of your life that are really none of their business?
- Do your friends dislike your partner?
- Have you ever made excuses to your friends about the way your new date treats you?
- Have you seen your partner lose their temper with anyone?
- Do you feel there could be some big secret they are keeping from you?
- After dating for some time, if your partner hasn't invited you back to their home, could they be hiding something? Like a spouse?
- Does your partner call when promised?
- Do you ever feel explosive anger toward your partner?
- Does your partner's generosity make you feel guilty?
- Do any aspects of your current partner's behavior remind you of bad aspects of your past partner(s)?

As well as their personality traits, consider their family backgrounds. Do they come from broken, volatile, or chaotic homes? Many people who come from such families can successfully take steps to change themselves, but if you are worried about some of your new partner's behavior and you also know they have a difficult past, you should be aware that this might not be the right person for you.

People can put up with a lot of bad treatment if they are desperate for a relationship, but this will almost always lead to an unhealthy partnership.

FOOLS RUSH IN

Some relationships start with intense infatuation that quickly becomes physical, while others progress more steadily and rationally. There's nothing wrong with strong physical attraction, but how you handle it can determine whether the relationship develops in a healthy or an unhealthy way. If things are too rushed, it could suggest that you or your partner are too eager, insecure, or impulsive.

Have you had sex before finding out whether your partner is dating someone else as well? Most people looking for long-term relationships want things to be exclusive before they leap into bed.

If this hasn't been established, you could find yourself getting upset when you discover that your partner has a date with someone else the night after you stayed over. The other problem is that once you are wearing lust-tinted glasses, they can blind you to any potential problems in the relationship. You'll have to wait until the lust fades to find out that you have anything else in common *besides* lust.

Comparing your core traits

In the early weeks of a relationship, you'll both be trying to accommodate each other and to discover what the other person's lifestyle is like. You can't manufacture situations to test your partner's core traits—nor should you—but you are bound to come across situations that indicate what they are really like. After a couple of months of dating, run through the seven core traits and values you listed in your dating notebook and see whether you think this person is truly compatible with you.

- Are they expressive when they hear about your good news? Do they leap up and punch the air, and talk animatedly about how much they are happy and proud of you? Or do they just nod with quiet satisfaction and not make a big deal of it? Do you react in similar ways when they come to you with good news? How about when you get bad news or have a stressful day? Do they know how to make you feel better? How about when they have had a bad day? Does their emotional style match yours? If so, that's a positive sign.
- How about their social style? Do you prefer to mingle independently at parties or stand side by side? Or would you both rather stay at home? You should be getting an idea of whether you are compatible in this area after a few weeks together.
- It can take longer than a few dates to assess another person's cognitive mode. Are they willing to read a book that you recommend if you say you found it particularly interesting? If there's a new exhibition that you want to see at a local gallery, are they happy to join you? Do you like to watch similar television programs most of the time?
- Falling for another person gives us a burst of energy, but you should be able to tell quite early on whether they are hard-working or more laid-back, sporty or cerebral, ambitious or happy-go-lucky. Do their physical energy levels seem roughly the same as yours?

Go over the areas that are most important to you and decide how well you match. No matter how crazy you feel about the other person now, your relationship will have less chance of lasting if there are major incompatibilities in three of your seven core traits and vital attributes. The mere act of reflecting on this is useful. Relationships are more often successful when people are attentive to them.

Are your vital attributes compatible?

- How similar are your backgrounds and upbringings? If you introduced your family to your partner's would there be common ground? Did you have similar religious upbringings? Did you come from a huge family or a small one? Being the same on these things is not critical, but having backgrounds in common can make it easier to understand each other.

- Relationship skills will emerge over the course of time rather than be apparent from the get-go, but make sure that you feel you are being listened to. Does your new partner tend to remember things that you told them are important to you? Do they respond appropriately to what you tell them? You should feel that your partner is being appropriately responsive to you. If something wonderful happens, your partner should want to celebrate. If something terrible happens, your partner should be there to support you. And you should be responding to your partner in a way they perceive as being appropriately responsive. When you are doing this, you are signaling that you understand your partner, you're validating their point of view, you're displaying that you care for them, and these factors all help to build intimacy.

Being appropriately responsive to your partner, and making sure they perceive it, is one of the most important skills you can have in a relationship.

- If you mention that you are nervous about a meeting with one of your company's clients the next day, it will make you feel very cared for if your partner gives you a quick call the following evening to see how the meeting went. It's not the end of the world if he or she forgets, but it's a nice gesture. Remember, no one will be able to respond in the perfect way on every occasion, but they should get it right most of the time. Look at overall patterns of responses rather than individual incidents. Be ready to cut your partner some slack if they have snubbed you because they got yelled at by their boss, but if it happens repeatedly something may be wrong.

- How is your ability to resolve conflict looking at this early stage? When you disagree over which kind of takeout food to get, or which show to watch on TV, is it always the same person who caves in, or are you able to negotiate? "We had Chinese last weekend because I felt like crispy duck pancakes, so I guess it's only fair that you get to choose this time. Why don't we always take turns?" If you got into a bigger fight, did one of you withdraw while the other one wanted to engage? Did your partner show contempt, or did you find yourself rolling your eyes? These can be signs that your conflict resolution styles are not compatible (for more on this, see pages 146–152).

- Where do you both stand on religion and politics? If neither of you feels particularly strongly about either, this should be fine, but if one person has strong beliefs that the other doesn't share, or vehemently disagrees with, this could be a major problem down the line.

Spend an hour thinking about each of these areas before letting the relationship get too serious. This shouldn't be a chore. When you are in the early weeks of dating a new person whom you like, you spend an inordinate amount of time thinking about them anyway, so you might as well make it productive thinking rather than just idle daydreaming or doodling their name on Post-It notes.

Your "must haves" and "can't stands"

Does your date check all three "must have" boxes for you? Are they free of your "can't stand" qualities? You may not be able to tell everything in the early weeks but you can begin to figure out whether you think you share the same type of goals for the future.

While it's a mistake to try and pin someone down on the marriage and kids questions too early in a relationship, it's only natural to talk about your long-term goals, dreams, and plans. They're part of who you are. If your date reciprocates and tells you their dreams, you will be able to judge whether your goals sound compatible.

For example, if the person you're dating wants to quit their job in six months to travel the world and work with the Peace Corps, that is valuable information to know as soon as possible. Or if your potential partner hates their job but has no plans to change it, you'll have to decide if their career unhappiness will negatively affect you and your relationship in the future. Also, by coming clean about your own vision of the future, you give your date the opportunity to decide whether or not they want to be in the picture with you.

Start the conversation by sharing some information yourself: "Five years from now, I really want to have written a novel, and with any luck had it published. How about you? Do you have any five-year goals?" Or "One day when I can afford it, I'd like to buy a place near a beach where I could go for weekends during the summer. What would your dream vacation home be?"

When it comes to the "can't stands," you can tell whether or not a person smokes from day one and it won't take long to figure out if they hog the remote when you watch TV. But more subjective qualities such as jealousy, or being tight with money, may only emerge over time. Watch for clues, but don't react too strongly to the odd occasion when they question a bill in a restaurant; if they do it virtually every time you eat out, take note and determine how much it bothers you.

If all the vital signs are looking good, and you're having lots of fun together it could be time to let the relationship get closer. But you still don't need to rush things. If this person is truly the right one for you, you have plenty of time to get to know each other and let the relationship grow naturally.

Getting intimate

Intimacy doesn't just mean sex (although sex is part of it); it also means emotional closeness. It's not something that should be rushed into, because it's important that a certain level of trust has formed between you. That can only develop gradually through spending time together. One partner might want to move faster than the other, but this need not be a problem so long as you are respectful of each other's point of view. At this stage, being open and honest, communicating your beliefs and desires clearly, and making sure both partners are heard and respected can set up a good pattern of communication for the relationship.

Here are some issues that might arise in the early weeks. Although everyone will handle these issues a little differently there are also some suggestions on how you can approach them to ensure sure you are communicating well and respecting each other's beliefs.

What should you do if your date wants sex before you are ready?

While you may be fearful about expressing your need to take things slowly, it's essential to your relationship success that you express your desires up front and keep the lines of communication open. Find a comfortable and safe environment in which to have a conversation about it. Put your potential partner at ease by letting them know how much you like them. Then take a deep breath, summon your inner strength, and communicate your needs. Your partner will most likely thank you for being up front and honest. In fact, by having this difficult discussion, you may deepen the level of intimacy between you.

It might be trickier if it's the woman who wants sex while the guy doesn't, but you should still have the conversation. Being able to set boundaries around something you do or don't want to happen is a good sign for the relationship; being strong-armed into something is not.

If you don't want to have sex until you get married, it's only fair to let the other person know very early on. Continually pushing them away without saying why is unkind and puzzling, and will damage any emotional trust that's developing.

When is it a good time to ask whether the relationship is exclusive?

One of the most difficult intimacy issues to discuss in any new relationship is the subject of exclusivity. Are we or aren't we? How soon is too soon? Is it safe to discuss or not? Talk about being exclusive on the first date is almost always too soon, but every couple is a little different. If you've been spending a significant amount of time together, are starting to talk about plans for the future, and are engaged in a deepening physical relationship, chances are good that it's time for a heart to heart about becoming exclusive with one another. Again, your partner will most likely appreciate your courage in taking a risk and addressing this important issue, and your intimacy will deepen.

When should you introduce them to your friends or family?
You will probably want the first few dates to be just about the two of you. No matter how much your loved ones are agitating to meet this new potential partner, make sure that the relationship is progressing well and that this is a person you would like to continue getting to know better. When you do meet up, try to do so in a natural way, on neutral territory, rather than wheeling them or her straight to your parents' house to sit across a dinner table and be cross-examined (for more on handling introductions to your loved ones, see pages 163–166).

Should the man always be the one to call and arrange dates?
Just as it's now totally acceptable for women to make the first move, it's also fine for them to call a man they're dating and say "Hey, do you want to catch a movie on Thursday night?" If one person is doing all the chasing—making the calls, sending texts, and choosing where you go on dates—it sets up an unhealthy dynamic of inequality. A long-term relationship is about both partners contributing rather than one trying to win over the other.

But remember that in the early weeks of a relationship both of you are trying to figure out if this is the right person to go out with, and the right relationship to pursue. You don't want to come across as desperate or clingy, and you don't want a partner who comes across that way either. Don't be afraid to be the one to suggest something to do, but try to keep the calling and arranging of dates fairly reciprocal.

You'll probably fall into a pattern in terms of the evenings you see each other and the times of day when you speak. Always return calls, texts, and emails that require a response, and be considerate of the other person's schedule. Also, remember that there are many *reasons why someone might not be able to call you back right away, especially during working hours. If you continually find yourself calling and not getting a response in a reasonable amount of time, take note.*

When should you share your deepest secrets?

We've all got a few skeletons in the closet, whether they're mistakes we've made in the past or ways in which we've been wronged by others. The idea of sharing them with a new partner can be terrifying. In most cases, you don't have to do it immediately. Wait until the time seems right, or until circumstances force the issue.

For example, it could be that you have problems trusting another person because of something that happened to you in the past. Have you ever discussed it with anyone? If not, talk to a trusted friend, family member, counselor, or therapist before sharing it with a potential partner you have only known for a short time. Your date will need to know at some stage, so that they can be sensitive to your issues. If they are the right person for you, and you explain to them clearly what happened and how it has affected you, it should deepen the relationship rather than damage it.

If you did something in your past that you are ashamed of—maybe you used to take drugs, or got a conviction for drunk driving— choose your moment to reveal it. If it's a particularly bad secret, it could spell the end of your relationship—we never know what might be a deal breaker for another person—or it could be accepted graciously. It's always better for your partner to hear it from you than from someone else, though.

True intimacy is built on being able to accept both the good and bad aspects of a partner. If this relationship is going to grow, you need to be willing to share some of those skeletons, but be sensitive and thoughtful about when you reveal them.

Is it too early to take a trip together?

Flying off to the Caribbean for a week away when you've only known each other for two weeks would be trying to run before you can walk. Vacations are stressful because of the weight of expectation we carry with us. There are numerous problems to solve as you negotiate airports, unfamiliar locations, different types of cuisine, potentially disappointing hotels, and unforeseen expenses. Yet, we all expect our trips together to be restful, stimulating, romantic, and perfect in every way.

Why are you trying to fast-track your relationship instead of enjoying taking it slowly, step by step? As with sex, people who try to rush into intimacy by going away together in the early days may be motivated by their insecurities. It's much better to take things gradually—a day trip, then a weekend—so you can check that your vacation styles are similar before you spend several months' rent on the trip of a lifetime.

Ultimately, intimacy is something that builds over time. In any romantic relationship, it's important to take things slowly, communicate your needs while working to meet the other person's needs, and build a level of trust you're both comfortable with.

Is it too soon to say "I love you?"

Most people who say the three magic words after two dates are living in a dream world. They may be strongly attracted to each other, but knowing if that person is right for the long haul takes longer to figure out. You should be wary when you hear these words during the first few weeks—or if you are tempted to say them yourself in the first few weeks—because it may be infatuation talking. And that infatuation may soon fade.

It's not a reason to walk away, but don't find yourself falling for honeyed words either. Move at a pace that feels right to you and hope that your emotional styles will meet up eventually.

What if it doesn't work out?

There are two ways you can take the failure of a relationship in the early stages. You can think: "I am unlovable, so it's not surprising that they dumped me. Basically I'm not worthy of a relationship." Or you can think: "They weren't the right person for me, so I need to get out there and start looking again."

If you take the "I got rejected because I'm unlovable" approach, it will be much harder to make your next relationship work. Even before the first date you are sabotaging it and setting yourself up for another failure. If this attitude is engrained in your psyche, you should find professional help to unravel where it comes from and take steps toward building a healthy sense of self-worth. This may be a long process, but it will be a valuable one. People who get into romantic relationships while feeling they are not worthy of one are more likely to find the relationship fails—or, worse yet, find a partner who takes advantage of them or is abusive.

If you take the attitude that they just weren't the right person for you, you're ready to move on and find someone with qualities that meet your needs more precisely. You didn't fail—the relationship did, and there can be all kinds of reasons why.

If your core values and attributes don't match up, it's best to move on sooner rather than later. Sometimes they might have been the right person but you met them at the wrong time—perhaps when one of you was fresh out of a long-term relationship and not ready for another, or just as you got a promotion that would take you to the other side of the country.

Whether you were the one to pull the plug, or the one on the receiving end of rejection, be realistic about it. If you think there are any specific lessons you can learn, jot them down in your dating book. Did you overlook one of your "must haves" or "can't stands?" Were your backgrounds too dissimilar? Or did you leap into bed on the first date and the spark fizzled out? Think about what you can do differently the next time, brush yourself off, and set about finding the next date. All of these lessons can make you a better person, and help you to find a better partner and build a better relationship.

Jen and Andy

Jen was working as a hotel receptionist in 1995. One night she was covering a co-worker's shift as a favor when Andy checked in as a guest. They hit it off and dated for a few months but, for one reason or another, things didn't work out. One year later, they reunited briefly but, once again, it didn't last. The funny thing was that neither of them forgot the other. They both held onto photos and memorabilia of their time together. Sometimes they thought about trying to get in touch again. Then, in January 2005, Jen was thinking of leaving eHarmony because she hadn't met a match, when she received an email one night—and it was from Andy. He had just signed up on the site and her profile was one of the first he received. They had both always felt that the other was "the one who got away," and by then they were ready to recognize the signs. They got married in January 2009 and are looking forward to their future together.

CHAPTER EIGHT

Making it Work

The weeks turn into months, you've agreed that you're exclusive, and all the signs are looking positive. Lucky you! The honeymoon phase of a relationship, when you think about each other constantly, feel totally, wonderfully alive in the other person's presence, and can't wait to rip your clothes off in your haste to get into bed, is an addictive stage. You are getting to know and love another human being and, what's more, they seem to be in love with you as well. You are walking on air, humming love songs under your breath, and feeling benevolence for the whole universe.

Not all relationships go through an infatuation stage, but many do. The passion that people experience during that time is a powerful motivation to stick with a new relationship during the early unstable months. Infatuation is driven, in part, by your biology and neurochemistry. It offers immediate rewards, and keeps us interested as the deeper connection that comes from understanding and being understood by another person develops. However, passion can make us see the other person as better than they are and overlook their flaws, so it's a good idea not to leap into any long-term commitments while you are still experiencing the rosy glow of the early stages.

Honeymoon phases don't have a set shelf life. They can come and go over the years as love grows and develops, so don't panic if you detect signs that your initial honeymoon phase is coming to an end: the first time your partner cancels a date because they've got too much work to finish for the next day; the first real argument; the first night you sleep together without having sex. Think of these as signs that the relationship is progressing rather than fizzling out.

As a relationship grows you should concentrate on making it deeper and stronger. There are several ways to keep strengthening the bond between you so that you grow closer together over the months and years, adding to the sum of shared experiences that form the glue that keeps couples together for the long term. Most of them are a learning process. By being aware of them, you should be able to improve your relationship skills over the years ahead.

BONDING EXPERIENCES
Try something that neither of you has tried before: a hot-air balloon flight, scuba diving, trekking in the Grand Canyon, or going to a jazz club. Novel experiences can build passion and intimacy in a relationship because in your head you attribute the excitement of the experience to the feeling of being with the other person. You're tricking your body in a way, but you are also creating a shared experience, which is unique to the two of you, and different from anything you have done with anybody else before.

Being responsive

We talked earlier about perceived responsiveness—the importance of feeling that your partner responds to you in a genuine and appropriate way most of the time. When you are responsive to your partner, you signal that you understand your partner, you're validating their point of view, and you're displaying that you care for them, which are all going to help to build intimacy between you.

Being responsive will make someone who is "anxiously attached" feel more secure and calm those who fear rejection, so they don't need to jostle for reassurance all the time. It will also help someone who is somewhat avoidantly attached feel more confident that they can expect responses that are pretty consistent over time.

There is another benefit to being responsive when you hear about a partner's good news—it results in positive emotions. There is a lot of evidence that positive emotions have a tendency to create an upward spiral: I do well, it makes me feel good, I'm more likely to try again, which makes me more likely to have another success, which makes me feel good, and so forth. This pattern also exists in relationships. If your partner is appropriately responsive toward you, it makes you feel better about the relationship and feel positive emotions. You care for the partner more, which makes the relationship more intimate. This makes you more likely to respond appropriately to them, which makes them feel better about themselves and the relationship, and so on and so on. This is an upward spiral that was started by responding well to your partner's good news.

> *The more responsive you are to your partner, the more likely it is that your responsiveness will be repaid, especially in the early stages of the relationship, when you are still laying the groundwork.*

Celebrating the good times

Everyone knows that it's important for couples to support each other during bad times, but did you know that it's maybe even more important to share in their triumphs and celebrate their good news?

Imagine that your partner has just finished a huge work project. It's gone very well, their boss is ecstatic, and is talking about a promotion. How do you react? Do you:

a) Hug and kiss your partner, break open some champagne, and spend half an hour chatting about how proud you are and how great it is.

b) Smile and nod at your partner's story. You are happy for them but you don't want to steal from their spotlight so you don't make a big deal out of it.

c) Point out the downsides of the good event or talk about your own big work project.

d) Just stay neutral and not engage very much in the conversation.

Your reaction may vary according to the mood you're in, the context of the conversation, or how well your relationship is going at that moment. But stop to consider what response you would want if you were the one brimming with good news to share. Of course you would want "a," and you'd feel hurt if you got "b," "c," or "d."

Studies have shown that the way in which spouses respond to each other's good news is directly correlated with how satisfied they are with their marriages—and this applies to relationships in earlier, pre-marriage stages as well. Even just the memory of their partners' enthusiastic responses makes people feel better about their relationships. That's pretty powerful stuff! Imagine what it could be like if you responded to your partner with genuine interest and enthusiasm each and every time they told you about a piece of good news, and they responded to you in the same way. These positive associations would accumulate over time, making your relationship stronger and more satisfying.

Here's how to show your partner that you are responsive:

- Be empathetic. Try to understand what they are thinking and feeling and view positive events from their perspective. Every time you make the effort to empathize, you reach a better understanding of your partner's meaning and strengthen your connection. Your partner will see that you are putting effort into understanding it from their point of view. And this better understanding will lead you to be able to react to your partner faster and more appropriately.

- Provide feedback that proves the message was understood. Pick up on part of it and ask appropriate questions. Ask for clarification if you don't understand something. Refer back to something relevant that was mentioned earlier. Show attentiveness with your eyes and your body language as well, so that your partner feels you are genuinely interested and not just faking.
- Be generous with supportive statements. When we give recognition to our significant others and genuinely compliment their achievements, we reassure them how important they are to us and make them feel better about themselves. And be sure to keep the focus on your partner; this is their time to shine in the spotlight.

When we are responsive to our partners, many of the other keys to good communication in a relationship fall into place naturally. Think of it as making little deposits in a savings account that will pay big dividends over time.

Support in bad times

You might think that the same lessons of appropriate responsiveness apply in bad times as in good, but this can be a touchier process, because there are different kinds of support needed for different occasions. If your partner receives bad news, they may not want you to empathize and join them in endless handwringing about how dreadful it is.

Let's say they've just heard that a big work project they've put a lot of effort into is being wound up because the boss doesn't think it's making enough money. How would you respond?

a) You might sit down and listen as they rant on about why their boss has made the wrong decision and how they would have made it profitable in the end.

b) You might make suggestions about how they could turn the situation around, perhaps by writing out a new business plan to prove that the project could be profitable within six months.

c) You might give them a hug, say how sorry you are, then make an especially nice dinner that evening, giving them their own space to work out their disappointment.

It's not always easy to see which is the most supportive response. The best response may be different each time and every person may not react well to the same response. Informational support (response "b") could lower your partner's self-esteem by making them feel they are not capable of taking care of the problem by themselves. Your behavior communicates the message: "You are not coping, but I will step in and take care of it for you." Emotional Support (response "a") may initially make it better by letting your partner vent, but if it goes on too long it may lead to ruminating on the bad outcomes instead of thinking about possible solutions.

You might think that response "c" is uncaring, but by giving your partner the space to think through the problem, you are demonstrating that you trust them to resolve it themselves. But this can also backfire if your partner expects you to take a more active role in your support. To give good support you need to know a lot about what your partner needs and how to provide it without making them feel badly about themselves.

Research has shown that the best kinds of support are the ones that are not even perceived by the other partner. For example, imagine one partner is studying for a hugely important professional exam. It's a stressful time and they are completely immersed in their work. The best kind of support would be for their partner to take over certain aspects of running the household, but without making a big deal out of it. They could do the dishes, take out the trash, pick up the dry cleaning and put it away in the closet, but without pointing out all that they were doing. Studies have shown that this kind of invisible support that goes below the radar won't undercut their partner's sense of self-esteem by making them feel they aren't managing, but will help the partner adjust to the stressful event by giving them more time to study for the exam. This isn't always possible, though. If you do give your partner visible support, offering an out for their ego may be in order. "You know what? I'm going to pay the bills, do the grocery shopping, and make all the dinners this month. Once you've passed your exam, you can do it for me for a month." That way you don't take away your partner's sense of being able to handle life. It becomes reciprocal rather than patronizing.

Conflict resolution

It's a popular myth that the goal of a perfect relationship is to be conflict-free. This isn't true. All long-term relationships will have some conflict. In fact, relationships in which partners never fight may be filled with repressed resentments that build up until they eventually explode over some minor trigger. Because partners in these types of relationships are not used to managing conflict on a regular basis, neither one has the skills necessary to solve the problems.

When you give support don't forget to make your partner feel good about themselves, without undercutting their self-esteem.

When couples can resolve conflict well it makes the relationship much easier but, like any other skill, when it is not used it can erode over time. So couples that avoid conflict just for the sake of avoiding conflict may leave issues festering, and at the same time reduce their ability to resolve them. When you hear someone boast "I didn't even complain when she left my iPod on the subway" or " I don't mind picking up his abandoned coffee cups with a film of mold on top," you are listening to someone who is in denial.

Second-time-around couples may argue more in the early stages of their relationship than fresh-faced youngsters because they are more set in their own opinions and ways of doing things. By your thirties, you will have formed your own social circles, domestic habits, and expectations of relationships, and it would be a miracle if another person arrived and shared exactly the same perspective. As you work out the structure of your lives together, there's going to be a certain amount of negotiation and compromise necessary and therefore there are plenty of issues that could spark arguments. The key is not to think of this as necessarily a bad thing but an opportunity to practice conflict resolution skills that will be beneficial to the relationship over the long term.

Trevor and Julie

Trevor had come out of a draining relationship in which he felt he was constantly giving support, while receiving little kindness in return. He wanted someone who would love him back, someone he could grow old with, and he decided to look for love online. Trevor and Julie were both in their fifties when they were matched by eHarmony. Their first telephone conversation lasted for three hours and they arranged their first date the very next day. Trevor clung to the fear that he was going to be taken for a fool once again, but he mustered the courage to meet Julie—and as soon as he met her he knew she was different. She was the supportive, long-term partner he was looking for and within two months he had proposed and been accepted.

Learning to argue well is one of the harder skills to master in a relationship, but when conflict is seen as a tool to move you toward a resolution and bring you together, it becomes something not to run away from but to embrace for the betterment of your relationship. Arriving at resolutions deepens your love and appreciation for each other and for what you share, and renews the desire to be with each other. That's why kissing and making up can be such fun!

How two people decide to manage their conflict can make all the difference between a relationship that works and one that ultimately doesn't.

However, there are certain warning signs that you need to watch out for in arguments because they can create an unhealthy pattern over time.

- Demand/withdrawal, where one person is engaging and demanding a conflict while the other is withdrawing or stonewalling, refusing to interact, is a sign of an unhealthy anxious/avoidant dynamic, which leaves both parties discontented (see page 29).

- Showing contempt for the other person is an indication that the relationship as a whole is not going well.
- Fighting dirty is never productive. There are boundaries you shouldn't cross or you could inflict a fatal wound on the relationship.

All of these signs bode poorly for the future of the relationship. The cumulative effect of bad conflict, yelling, tears, contempt, and stonewalling, happening once a month, or every time you have a fight, will put an impossible strain on your feelings for each other over the months and years (if you get that far).

Learning to fight fairly is something that takes time and practice, but there are certain steps you can follow to help along the way. First of all, before you begin to talk about the actual subject of the conflict, step back and agree to set the following ground rules:

- No raising of voices—it's hard to talk constructively when someone is yelling.
- No sarcasm or put-downs—you are both mature adults who do not need a referee to assign blame and declare a "winner."
- Be specific to shed some light on what you are thinking and how you are feeling. Use "I" statements rather than "you" statements. Instead of saying "You are like this, and it drives me nuts!" you could say: "When you do this one activity, it makes me feel like this because…"
- If you can, schedule a rain check if there is alcohol involved. It's not usually a good idea to have serious discussions after one or both partners have been drinking. Alcohol will reduce your inhibitions and make you more likely to say something you didn't mean in the heat of the moment. And even though you may feel more relaxed in some ways, there comes a tipping point with alcohol in which people become emotionally unavailable, whether they are aware of it or not.

Now follow the three steps below to try and reach a resolution of the conflict.

1. Stop and listen

When a heated situation comes up, the first step toward resolving it is simply to stop talking (or yelling) and make sure you know why your partner is upset. This isn't always easy to do during the heat of an argument, but if you can keep yourself from yelling you may find that you can get to resolve the conflict faster than if you kept yelling. Make sure you understand what a successful resolution is for your partner (or in other words, what they want in the situation). And don't be afraid to restate what you think they are communicating to you in a factual manner. Again, spare the sarcasm and confirm that you fully understand them. Even in the middle of an argument you still should respect your partner's opinion, even if it is not your own. You don't have to agree with their point of view, but you do have to understand it in order to come to a resolution, so let your partner correct you if they feel your take on the situation is slightly off.

> *To be able to listen with complete attentiveness to your partner is one of the highest expressions of love; you accept them as they are, despite differing points of view.*

The goal is to foster the freedom of mutual honesty with your partner. You shouldn't bury problems and, equally as important, neither should your partner; everyone needs to be heard and understood. If you sense they are burying feelings simply to end an argument quickly, encourage them to open up. Remember, just as you have a right to your own thoughts and feelings, so does your partner.

2. It's your turn

When you feel you understand your partner's point of view, it is your turn to lay out your position, and to do it as calmly as you can. They should afford you as much respect and attentiveness as you provided to them. Should they slip in that regard, gently remind them. One responsibility in love is to teach one another how to be better people, so exercise compassion for your partner as they learn how to sharpen communication skills to be able to communicate more effectively with you. The same goes for partners who are unwilling to try problem-solving techniques or who may seem unwilling to try anything new that might help the relationship—you'll have to set a good example by employing effective conflict management skills when arguments arise and hope they will follow your lead.

Finally, if your partner does not restate your position once you have finished expressing your point of view, ask them to tell you in their own words what they think you are trying to communicate.

3. Compare and resolve

Even if you are not any calmer, you both will now have a detailed understanding of what happened and why the other person is upset. It may even be that the two of you have found out that the conflict was a simple misunderstanding that is easily hashed out. But if you still have a disagreement, you can move toward trying to resolve the issue because you both know what that resolution looks like. Of course, there may be disagreements that do not have a mutually acceptable resolution, but making sure you understand each other ensures that both of you will feel as if your point of view has been heard and respected, rather than the argument breaking down into misunderstandings and hurt feelings.

THE DO'S AND DON'TS OF FIGHTING FAIRLY

- Do listen attentively and ask questions to clarify your partner's point of view.
- Don't resort to sarcasm, yelling, and immature name-calling.
- Do take a rain check on resolving the conflict if alcohol is involved, or if you are overly tired or hungry.
- Don't run away from conflict. A resolution rarely falls into place on its own.
- Don't drag older issues into the argument for the sake of adding weight to your position.
- Do steer clear of sensitive areas that will escalate the fight.
- Don't expect you or your partner to become master communicators overnight. It takes time and practice.

Apologies and forgiveness

If you can resolve conflict fairly, you have removed one of the things that could chip away at the relationship over the years. However, if you have stepped over the line in some way, a quick and sincere apology is a powerful tool. Blast them with honesty.

"I was tired and stressed and I said something I didn't mean to say. I'm sorry."

"I meant to [do that thing you asked me to do] and it slipped my mind. I'll try my best to make sure it never happens again."

"I know that is a sensitive issue for you and I'm sorry that I brought it up."

If you are the recipient of an apology, you need to learn to forgive and move on. Major transgressions will be harder to forgive, but harboring grudges is a poison that eats into the relationship over time. If you have an issue that you are having trouble resolving, it's worth considering relationship counseling for some independent, wise advice.

Dealing with annoying behavior

Perhaps he always leaves his socks on the floor; maybe she always interrupts you when you're on the telephone; you find it disrespectful that he is often late to meet you; you hate it when she expects you to do a task without giving you all the information you need to complete it. For the sake of peace and quiet, is it better to let the little things slide and not make an issue out of them? The answer is a resounding "No!" According to eHarmony research, confronting the issue with your partner will benefit your relationship.

Early in a relationship, you might view your partner through rose-tinted glasses, happily unaware of or ignoring the other's irritating little foibles. As you spend more time together, these previously innocent behaviors can start to grate a bit more. Although they may not lead to outright conflict, they are related to lower levels of satisfaction with the relationship as a whole.

We all do things that annoy our partners and the more you are annoyed by your partner, the worse your relationship may get. However, if you are able to express your annoyance, the situation doesn't get any worse. It's like a little release valve that takes the pressure out of things. It might not stop your partner from doing that thing you hate, but it makes you feel better to tell them about it. It may even stave off an argument later down the line.

In a survey of 1,036 married couples, 40 percent of people, male and female, said their partners had done something to annoy them during the last twenty-four hours. However, wives who expressed their annoyance to their husbands reported higher levels of marital satisfaction than those who didn't. In addition, husbands who expressed their annoyance had wives who reported higher levels of marital satisfaction. In other words, wives expressed greater satisfaction if they expressed their own annoyance, and if their husbands expressed annoyance with them. It means that the communication channels are working.

Being able to talk about issues and areas that annoy you is a sign that you are committed, comfortable, and open with your partner.

Moreover, being open and confronting issues with your partner could make you live longer than if you internalize your anger. In recent studies, those who kept their feelings to themselves were more likely to die sooner than those who spoke out. This is at least partly because internalizing anger is stressful and promotes the release of stress hormones in the body, causing increased heart rate, faster breathing, tense muscles, and various other reactions. This reaction is important in an emergency because it prepares you to react quickly, but when you repeatedly experience stress reactions over a period of time, they can cause major damage to your health. Letting your feelings out and having an argument might feel difficult at the time, but it could act as a release valve. Once the conflict is resolved, you will no longer be stressed and your body can get back to normal.

CRITICIZING WITH KINDNESS

Expressing your annoyance doesn't mean it's open season to belittle your partner. Surveys show that women are more likely to be harsh in the way they criticize. Try to practice the "soft start-up" where you begin with some statement of kindness or compassion before following up with the criticism. For example: "I know you are really tired at the moment, but it would be great if you could drop your socks into the laundry basket when you take them off." Or: "I appreciate that you are trying to be helpful when you interrupt my phone calls to remind me of something, but I find it difficult to have two conversations at once. Would you mind telling me after the call is finished?"

Fanning the flames of lust

Does this sound familiar? In the early weeks of a relationship, you can't keep your hands off each other. You are counting the hours until you can be alone together so you can make love. As time goes by, though, the chemistry seems to fizzle out a bit and, before you know it, a few days, even a couple of weeks, have gone by without any sex. Either that or you find yourself feeling disengaged during the act. Differing levels of sexual desire can be magnified by age, so this is a problem that may be more common among second-time-around couples. But whatever you do, don't panic. It is quite common as relationships progress for sexual desire and satisfaction to decrease. It doesn't mean you should stop trying to keep the passion alive, though, because sex is a wonderful expression of intimacy in a relationship.

Recent research has suggested that one way to prevent a decrease in sexual desire is to adopt "approach-oriented goals" as opposed to "avoidance-oriented ones." Approach goals are focused on obtaining a good result. For example, having sex "to express love for your partner" is an approach sexual goal, whereas having sex "to prevent angering or upsetting your partner" is an avoidance sexual goal. Similarly, "wanting to deepen your relationship with your partner" is an approach relationship goal, whereas "wanting to make sure nothing bad happens to the relationship" is an avoidance relationship goal. In other words, approach goals want something good to happen and avoidance goals don't want anything bad to happen.

Seduce your partner because you love them, not because you're scared of losing them.

Everyone has their own unique style for both of these dimensions. For example, it's possible to be high in approach goals and avoidance goals at the same time. Research has shown that people who are high in approach and low in avoidance tend to feel better about themselves and their relationship. Those who are highly engaged with others out of a sense of enjoyment and growth are the most satisfied, and they tend to be able to extend the good times and weather the bad times. Everyone who has been in a long-term relationship knows that there are good days and bad days; sometimes life brings difficult situations, and sometimes we just don't feel as engaged with our partner as at other times. And these ups and downs inevitably take their toll on our sex lives.

If it is one of those days when your partner is really getting on your nerves, usually the last thing you want to do is have sex. However, highly approach-oriented people tend not to let these bad days affect their sexual desire nearly as much as other people. People who enjoy reaching out in order to strengthen their relationship have much more resilient sex lives. Even during hard times, they continue to enjoy the unique bond that sex brings to a relationship. On the other hand, there are some days when you and your partner just "click," and these times usually come with heightened sexual urges. Again, highly approach-oriented people are more likely to take advantage of these good days and feel even greater sexual desire.

While we may not all be approach-oriented at our basic core, we can take the time to reach out to our partners with a positive and caring intention. We can plan a day at the beach or take the time to meet for lunch just to show each other we really do care. And in demonstrating to each other our enjoyment in the other's happiness and satisfaction, we are building the kind of relationship where a dynamic sex life will flourish.

SPARK IT UP

If you feel that your sex life has hit a rut, try something new. This needn't mean buying sexy lingerie or adopting unusual techniques (unless this is something you both feel inclined to try). Instead, go somewhere you don't usually go, either for an evening or a long weekend. Try skinny-dipping in a lake. Sleep in a different bed. Have a massage together. Play footsie under the table at dinner. Shower together. Change your normal routine in some way—and don't forget to flirt.

Sex isn't the only important way of connecting. There will be times when you and your partner will want to keep the physical connection open by indulging in plenty of affectionate, non-sexual touching. Hugging, stroking of the head, a quick kiss, a neck massage— all of these have stress-reducing effects and can increase intimacy between partners.

Individuals have differing levels of need for physical affection, and it's good if your needs and your partner's are similar. If they are wildly different, it could mean you are on different paths in the relationship. However, if you are responsive to your partner's needs for touch and they are responsive to yours, your patterns could grow together over time.

Strategies for a successful relationship
With divorce statistics indicating that around 40 percent of marriages will fail in the West, no one can give you a cast-iron guarantee that your love will last forever. But if you are prepared to put in the groundwork and place a priority on continuing to work on your relationship, your chances will be better than most. Here are some strategies that surveys show will help make your relationship stronger.

Express gratitude
Saying thank you for any thoughtful things your partner does for you, such as running an errand, buying your favorite type of cheese, or simply bringing you a cup of coffee in bed, can help to strengthen your relationship. In a University of North Carolina study, partners were asked to keep track of the other's kind gestures, then participate in a "thanking task" in the laboratory. Afterward, gratitude was found to be positively associated with relationship quality and satisfaction for both men and women.

It's basically another case of responsiveness. Gratitude helps us to "find, remind, and bind" to each other's needs, triggering a series of emotions that make the other person feel good about themselves, and more connected to the relationship. It helps to build mutually responsive patterns.

The key is to feel a sense of appreciation for your partner's good will rather than indebtedness. Those who feel they "owe" their partner might not experience the self-esteem boost that simple gratitude can bring. So if your romantic other does something nice for you, be sure to say thanks—and mean it.

OPPOSITE-SEX FRIENDSHIPS

Seeking emotional comfort and intimacy with members of the opposite sex other than your partner can create an unhealthy pattern in your relationship. You may already have had a number of friends of the opposite sex when you went into your second-time-around relationship, but be careful how you continue these friendships so as not to arouse jealousy and misunderstandings. Even if they are not remotely romantic, opposite-sex friendships can be very intimate, and you will need to handle the situation delicately until your new partner understands the situation and trusts you both. You will probably find you end up seeing less of your opposite-sex friends anyway, as you balance the demands of your relationship with those of your existing social network. (There's more on this on the opposite page.)

Be on the lookout for unhealthy patterns

Couples develop habits in the way they interact with and treat each other. While some of these habits can be good (ending the day with a goodnight kiss, cuddling up when watching TV, sitting outside together to see the sunset), some can be detrimental. For example, if you adopt a condescending tone in communicating with your spouse ("Are you serious? You really thought Canaletto was a type of pasta?"), put them down in front of others ("Don't ask her—she can't even switch on the computer."), or start to take them for granted ("Why haven't you fixed the leaky washer in the bathroom? That's your job."), cracks can soon settle in. Listen to the tone you use with each other and treat the other person as you would like to be treated.

Make time for each other

When you met, you probably had a full life already, with work, a home to run, friends and family to keep up with, and other social and leisure commitments to fulfill. Now, here is a new person looking for several hours a week of your time. How can you possibly manage it?

The truth is that if you want a fulfilling relationship you need to prioritize it. Compare schedules at least once a week and carve out the quality time you are going to spend together. When that time comes around, put down your laptop, step away from the phone, and recommit your love, affection, and attention to each other. By making meaningful moments happen on a regular basis, you'll reconnect to your partner, deepen your intimacy, and realize just how precious the time you spend together can be. This can be very hard when you have a family, work, and friends, but the time you spend together will pay off for your relationship down the road...

Maintain your own identity

... But don't completely drop your friends, your tennis club, or other activities you enjoy, such as reading novels. You may not have as much time to devote to them, but don't let them slide entirely. While it's important to nurture your romantic relationship, it's also a huge mistake to expect a partner to fulfill all your needs. No one person can possibly nurture you emotionally and intellectually, while keeping you fit and healthy at the same time! If you drop all your independent interests, what are you going to have to talk about when you see each other?

By maintaining a life of your own throughout your relationship, you retain a sense of individuality, have more to share with your partner, and avoid any kind of feeling that you are missing out because some of your ever-changing needs, wants, and desires are not being met.

Keep the lines of communication open

If you are able to discuss openly and honestly any issues that arise, if you learn how to argue fairly, and manage one another's emotional expectations, you and your partner will be better equipped to weather any relationship storm ahead. The fact is that during any long-term partnership, there will be bumps in the road. The goal is not to avoid them, but to learn how to navigate them.

Communication can slip away before you even notice it. The rest of life can keep you from stopping and really listening to each other. If this happens, you may be able to open up the lines of communication by reaching out. Start by sitting down and saying something non-judgmental, such as: "We haven't been very close recently. I know I've been preoccupied with work issues, but what's going on with you?"

It will take emotional courage to open up the subject, but asking your partner about their needs and wants and explaining your own can go a long way to bridging any gap between you. Simply having the conversation will bring you closer together. And by asking for what you need, you may actually get it!

Don't forget to keep practicing the communication skills we discussed earlier, such as properly celebrating your partner's successes, or making sure you understand their point of view in an argument. If you continue to follow all this advice, you will find that communication is less likely to fade away.

Choose happiness over your need to be right

Would you rather be right, or would you rather be happy? The people who would rather be right constantly nag, belittle, and fight their partner over every tiny thing. Do you want to be that person, or would you like to be the kind of person whose relationship is blissful because you've let go of the need always to have the last word, come up with the right answer, or to prove your partner wrong? Conflict and arguments are going to be necessary sometimes, but there are times when it is better to let the small stuff go.

THE ART OF THE WELL-CHOSEN COMPLIMENT

If you are always saying "You look gorgeous, darling" or "That meal was delicious," your compliments can lose their impact. Aim to find a fresh one to give your partner at least once a week. Make them specific, and personal, and true. Some examples:

- "That phone call could have been tricky, but I thought you handled it really well."
- "I don't know how you remembered that. You've got a great memory!"
- "Your roast chicken is by far the best I've ever tasted."

It's complicated bringing a new person into your life, someone who wants to spend a lot of time with you, possibly with a view to creating a future together. In second-time-around relationships, there can be a range of extra complications that might not have arisen the first time. In the next chapter, we'll look at ways in which you can navigate some of the most tricky second-time-around problems to keep your relationship heading in a positive direction.

CHAPTER NINE

Special Challenges the Second Time Around

The second time around, you will probably already have created a home of your own, established a social network, and you may have had children with your previous partner. You will have formed your own ideas about politics, religion, and the radio station you like to listen to in the car. You will have set routines—gym on Tuesday and Saturday, gardening work on Sunday afternoon, holidays with your sister and her family, an annual yoga weekend with your best friend. No matter how excited you feel about your new partner, there are going to be moments when you resent giving up your established patterns in order to accommodate them. Why can't they just fit in with your ways?

During the first few months—even the first year—of a second-time-around relationship, there will be a bit of jostling for position as you establish whether things are going to be done the way you like them, the way your partner prefers, or some other way completely. Usually you spend more time in one partner's home than the other's, perhaps because there's more space, or it's more conveniently located for work. If it's your place, do you offer some hanging space in the closet and shelf space for toiletries, or do you prefer your partner to arrive with an overnight bag and take their things home again the next day? It should be easy to adjust your cooking repertoire to take account of the fact that they love spicy food and have a passionate dislike for broccoli. These are the kind of minor accommodations that most of us make without batting an eyelid, but there are other, more difficult compromises that will have to be worked out as the relationship progresses, and the way you deal with them will be a key indicator of how well things are going between the two of you.

> *You need to be open to change in all kinds of areas when you invite another person to become part of your life.*

One of the first issues that will raise its head is how to find time in your already full schedule to see your new partner—possibly on two or more evenings a week. Chances are that your friends and family will have to step aside and see a bit less of you than they've been used to. If they want you to be happy, this shouldn't be a problem, but you can be sure they will be scrambling to meet the new person who's whisked you away. They're bound to be curious, if nothing else. When and how you arrange this are issues that deserve some careful consideration.

Introducing your new partner to your friends and family

Be prepared for the first introductions to be stressful. For you, there may be a lot riding on it. You want all the people you love to get along with your new partner, because that will validate your choice of partner and make life a lot easier for everyone. You also want your partner to like your friends because they are a reflection of you and the choices you've made in your life. But they are all separate individuals with their own points of view, and it's not a given that everyone will automatically hit it off.

Try your best to help everyone to find some common ground. Introduce your partner first to the people you think they will have the most interests in common with, and not necessarily the ones you are closest to. Organize tickets for events that you will all find enjoyable. At a large gathering of your friends, try to give your partner a role that will make them feel involved, such as taking a turn on the barbecue or acting as the bartender. You know the friends who are likely to prove trickiest to win over, so take special care about the way you introduce them to your new partner.

There are several reasons why your friends could have mixed feelings about your new relationship. If they have always known you as part of a couple with your ex, and they still get along with your ex, you could be presenting them with a dilemma. Should they risk upsetting your ex by socializing with your new partner? Where should their loyalties lie?

These are questions your friends will have to resolve for themselves, but if they genuinely care about you, they will want you to be happy and will give the new person in your life a chance. You can make it easier for them by offering not to bring your new partner to particularly sensitive occasions that your ex will be attending, such as the wedding of a mutual friend. If your ex's feelings are still raw, it's kind to give them time to heal rather than rubbing their noses in the fact that you've been the first to meet someone new. Once you're both with someone else, it may be manageable for you all to attend the same event unless the relationship ended horribly (for advice on difficult exes, see page 167–168).

> *The more your social world works against the success of your relationship, the more difficult that relationship is going to be.*

If you have had a string of disastrous relationships in the past and been badly hurt, it's only natural for your friends to look critically at your new partner, trying to discern any signs that they could hurt you again. This is fine, so long as they aren't too obvious in their analysis. Well-meaning friends may take the new partner aside for a quiet word—"Hurt our friend and you'll have to deal with us." Statements such as this will only add to the pressure your new partner already feels.

If your friends are uneasy about your new partner—"Are you really sure they are right for you?"—how much weight should you give to their opinions? How does their disapproval reflect on your choice of partner? Does it mean there is some flaw in the relationship that will make it unlikely to last? Remember, however, that our friends and family are better predictors of whether a relationship will work or not for us than we are.

If only one or two of your friends or family feel this way, they may have personal reasons for the disapproval. Maybe your partner reminds them of someone they had a bad experience with. Maybe they are worried that they'll see less of you now that you're part of a couple again. But if most or all of your friends seem wary, it should plant a seed of doubt in your mind. If you're getting negative feedback from all sides, there may be some truth in their judgments. Remember, your friends and family will have your best interests at heart. Try to step back and see what they are seeing and work out if their objections are issues that could threaten the long-term stability of the relationship.

While involved in a relationship that's less than perfect, we're often afraid to admit that the negatives might be true—especially if we were single for a long time and it took us ages to meet anyone at all. Negative feedback doesn't mean you need either to break off with your partner or give up seeing your family and friends. Take the time to think about how any negative qualities your partner has may affect you in the future, but at the same time, be aware that your friends may change their tune when they get to know your partner better and see that the relationship is withstanding the test of time.

Ultimately, you have the final power of decision-making about whom you choose to have in your life. Listen to all the opinions and weigh them up alongside your own instincts. The better the decisions you make for yourself, the happier you will be, and the happier you are, the more you can share that happiness with someone who is perfect for you. It's another of those upward spiral situations.

Your new partner might not be as good at entertaining a crowd with witty anecdotes as your ex was. They might not earn as much, or have such a nice home. But if they make you happy, that's the most important thing.

Steve and Sue

Sue had been married for ten years and Steve for twenty, and when their marriages ended, both Sue and Steve found themselves living alone with few single friends and few dating possibilities. Sue lived with her two daughters, who were both teenagers with very busy social lives, and she realized she had become a taxi service that accommodated their lives. With the encouragement of her children, she decided that it was about time she got her own life back on track. Shortly after she made the decision to get back into the dating world, she met Steve on a relationship site. He was the honest man she had been looking for and when they met there was an instant spark between them. Sue believes that although her life was mapped out for her to a certain extent, she did have the power to change things, and because she made the decision to get out there and look for love again, she managed to become the master of her own destiny.

Dealing with the exes

Frankly, any relationship in which an ex-wife or ex-husband is still in the picture, whether because of proximity, child custody, or ongoing financial arrangements, can be difficult to navigate. Make sure that your new partner hasn't rushed into a relationship too soon; watch out for tell-tale signs such as photos on the mantelpiece, or the ex's name coming up in conversation rather frequently—even if it is preceded by expletives. If you think they are not really ready for a new relationship, it's worth having a conversation about it and perhaps distancing yourself for a while until all the lingering emotions have been worked through.

If the ex is playing manipulative games over alimony or custody of the kids, don't get involved. It's not your business. Comfort your partner if they are upset, but leave them to fight their own battles. This is not the Wild West and you don't have to ride out for a showdown at the OK Corral. Always remember that no matter how terrible the ex sounds, there is always another side to every story. Don't ever encourage your partner to break custody arrangements, or tell the kids poisonous stories about their other parent's behavior. Be the calm, stable, good guy in the scenario.

At some stage, you will have a conversation with your new partner about why their previous relationships didn't work out and how they ended. It's interesting to hear that his wife went off sex after the kids were born, or that her husband couldn't hold down a job for longer than a few months, or whatever the reason might be. It gives you a clue about what they might consider to be relationship-breaking behavior, and whether they are the type that does the leaving or the type that gets left.

You will pick up some information from their version of events, but don't assume you're getting the whole story, by any means. They're only human, and likely to airbrush over any aspects that cast them in a less than angelic light. Remember that relationships are complex, multi-faceted arrangements with nuances that no one outside the couple concerned will ever appreciate.

Dating a cheater

If your new partner cheated on their last partner that could have an impact on your relationship with each other. If they were capable of deceiving and hurting someone they cared about, it's worth stopping to ask a few questions to try and assure yourself that they won't do the same to you:

- Do they acknowledge they shouldn't have done it, no matter what extenuating circumstances there may have been?
- Do they accept responsibility for hurting the other people involved?
- Do you feel they learned something from the experience and that they will act differently in the future?
- Have they had any therapy, either couple's or individual therapy, to help them understand why they acted the way they did?

- Will you worry that they will cheat on you? If you are an anxious type, prone to worrying about where your partner is when they're not with you, then dating someone with a cheating history is not a great idea.

Most people don't want to cheat, but the situation they were in drove them to it. Once they are in a different situation, that problem may not arise again. However, if someone has cheated repeatedly in the past, they are more likely to cheat again in the future and are not a great bet as a partner.

> ### When a man leaves his wife to marry his mistress, a job vacancy has been created.

Listen to your gut instinct. If you think they have changed and they won't cheat again the next time because they found the whole situation so painful, then you may be fine. If you think they still feel they were justified in cheating because of their partner's neglect, there's a chance they could do it to you, no matter how much you dote on each other at the moment. There are bound to be periods in the future when things feel flat and dull between you, and you don't want to find yourself sneakily checking the messages on their mobile phone, or creeping downstairs in the middle of the night to look through their email inbox.

What if you were the one who cheated? Think through all the ramifications—the people you lied to, the hurt you caused to your ex-partner and your children (if you have any), the difficult position in which you put the person you cheated with, the friends who may have compromised themselves to back up your alibis—and realize that it was all very bad dating karma. What goes around tends to come around in some way. You might have to face the fact that someone could decide not to pursue a relationship with you now because you cheated before.

But it is important to remember that no one is destined to cheat. Every relationship is different and the unique set of circumstances that lead one of you to cheat will most likely be different this time around. If you have started a great relationship with someone who cheated before and you are worried, you need to be open and honest with them about your concerns. Remember: no one wants to cheat and ruin a great relationship, and it is possible to learn lessons from that past behavior. Was the cheating because communication had broken down? Then make sure to take time to keep talking. Was it promoted by many long business trips? Maybe you can go along on a few of them so you won't be apart for so long. You may find that those strategies make you feel more secure and make the relationship stronger.

Cheating is not unique to second-time-around dating, of course, but there will be a higher percentage of messy ends when you both have a dating history. Make sure you have thought through any misgivings you have about a new partner, either because of what you know about their past, or based on your friends' and family's judgments, and be sure you want to proceed with the relationship before you take the next step—letting them meet your kids.

Introducing your new partner to your kids

Having a new adult in their life is never casual for children, and if you introduce them to a string of people you only end up dating for a few weeks each, they will be confused. eHarmony experts recommend that any new relationship should be exclusive for several months (that is, a serious relationship and not a casual affair) before the partner is introduced to the children.

The way your children react to you dating again after splitting up with their other parent will depend on a number of things:

- Their age
- The character of the individual child

- How recent the divorce or break-up was
- How traumatic the break-up was for them
- The relationship they have maintained with each of their parents
- How secure they feel
- And the way you handle the introduction to your new partner.

When you feel the time is right, keep the first meeting low key and brief, and do all you can to remove pressure from everyone concerned. Don't expect them all to be best buddies after having a burger together. Your kids need as much time as you did to get to know someone new.

WHEN MEETING YOUR NEW PARTNER'S KIDS...

- Do ask about their interests and try to find common ground with them.
- Do bring a small gift for them if you are visiting their home.
- Do keep it light and fun and easy-going.
- Don't kiss and hug your partner excessively in front of them.
- Don't expect the kids to kiss and hug you.
- Don't attempt to discipline them. It's not your job.
- Don't expect to sleep in the same bed as your partner. It may take some time for the kids to get used to the idea that you sleep together.
- Do leave them with your partner at the end of the first meeting, instead of the two of you heading out to dinner and leaving them with a babysitter. It's symbolically important you aren't seen to be taking their parent away from them.

If your new partner doesn't have kids, realize that they may not know how to talk and act around young children, and may not understand what kind of conversational level is age-appropriate. Remember that you didn't become a parent overnight—you had nine months to get used to the idea. As time goes on and they come to visit you at home, give them some hints on breaking the ice, while not getting anyone's backs up:

"John is crazy about Lego and you could offer to give him a hand with his new starship."; "Be sure to tell Evie you like her dress."; "Don't attempt to go into Callum's bedroom. No one's allowed in there."

A gradual approach allows children to adjust to their parents' dating (and the new dating partner) at a pace that allows for successful parenting.

With the US divorce rate lingering at around 40 percent for first marriages, many children have experienced their parents' divorce by the time they are eighteen. And most adults will start dating again within a year after their divorce—which is great for them, but can take a lot of adjustment for their kids. Don't feel you have to be single and celibate just because your children won't accept someone else. They don't have the right to make that decision for you. But don't force them kicking and screaming to accept a new "mommy" or "daddy," or you could do a lot of psychological damage. Here are just a few of the issues you may have to confront, depending on the ages of the children.

The under-fives
Children under the age of five can be pretty adaptable. They will be concerned about how a new partner is going to affect them, but if they arrive bearing gifts and they are ready to get down on the floor and play, it shouldn't rock their world too badly. You may find that a young child will try to sit between you and your partner as you watch TV, and might try to clamber into bed between you. They want to establish that even if you have someone new in your life, they are still the most important person to you. It's wise to let them do that, in whichever ways feel most appropriate.

Aged five to ten
One study found that children between the ages of five and ten are more possessive of their mothers than older children, and it can be

very stressful for them when she begins dating. They have their own issues of loss, betrayal, adjustment, and trust to deal with, and they may still be working through these issues long after you are over the break-up yourself. Parents need to make sure that children understand their continued importance to them and give them freedom to carry on a loving relationship with their other parent (despite any personal misgivings).

WEEKEND DADS

Children of all ages may have more trouble adjusting to their fathers' new relationships than to their mothers'. This could be because custody arrangements mean they see less of Dad and they want all of his time to themselves when they do meet. Leaving him on a Sunday evening while knowing that he will be spending a large part of the week with someone new can be especially difficult, since they fear losing him. New partners should be sensitive to this and let children have plenty of time on their own with their dad, instead of feeling like they need to join in on every last activity.

If the relationship was the cause of their parents' divorce and kids know this, they're going to be prejudiced against a new partner from the start. They may blame the new partner even if it is unjustified, so meeting them for the first time will bring up many emotions. Sticking to neutral turf will help, and an activity, such as bowling, a boat trip, or a visit to a theme park, can help to break the ice.

When the kids are between the ages of five and ten it's a particularly tricky time to bring someone new into your life, and you risk that your child will resent the newcomer if things are not handled very sensitively. These age ranges are not hard and fast, however, and you could easily find older or younger children taking it badly and your eight-year-old taking it completely in his stride.

Teenagers

Teenage children are entering a new world of dating and will be directly influenced in their behavior by the way you act. What they see is what they'll do. Research has shown that single parents'—and especially mothers'—attitudes and behaviors around sex directly influence their children's. Make sure you have had a conversation with them about appropriate behavior for adults and adolescents before either side starts an intimate relationship.

Tread carefully if you have been single for a while and a new partner threatens to usurp your kid's role in the house; for example, if you are a woman with a teenage son who is used to being "the man of the house," your new partner shouldn't charge in and take over any jobs your son traditionally did, such as washing the car; similarly, if a teenage daughter has been looking after her dad for a while, she might not be pleased when a new woman comes in and helps him to choose his clothes.

On the whole, though, teenagers will be far more concerned about their own social world than yours. You are over the hill, and to them it's pretty gross that you are kissing and even having sex with someone else, but so long as it doesn't change their curfew time, it's no big deal.

Adult children

Sometimes grown-up children can create a whole new set of issues when they try to "parent" their parents. Whether you were bereaved or your marriage ended in divorce, they may idealize your ex and resent any "replacement." They might not speak out until (or unless) you announce your engagement, but they could sabotage you in other, subtler ways, such as coming up with odd objections or being unwilling to help you make the time to date.

If your past relationships have ended badly, your kids may be concerned that the same thing will happen again. Even if you don't have a history of difficult, troubled relationships, it's quite common for adult children to fear that their parents will be taken in by a con artist (male or female). If it's been many years since you dated, it's important to understand that much more caution is required now than was when you dated in the past. If a date you barely know asks you for money, don't ever give it; chances are, they're up to no good. Similarly, don't give anyone your bank details or email password or burglar alarm code until you are very sure about them. Explaining to your children that you understand this may help to alleviate their fears somewhat.

Perhaps they are scared that you will get hurt again, either through a break-up or another bereavement. To someone who is thirty-five, a three-year relationship that ends in the death of a partner may seem like a catastrophe. To someone who is seventy-five, a three-year relationship that ends in the death of a partner may seem like a sad, sweet, life-affirming blessing and well worth the pain.

> *Explain to your children the different perspective that age brings, and help them to see that you are happy to accept some risk in return for the joy that a romantic relationship can bring.*

The best remedy for any and all concerns your adult children have is a serious heart to heart. It may be difficult to have this conversation, but it is vital. Many adult children still haven't quite come to terms with the fact that their parents are real people who need companionship, intimacy, and sex. Explain to them that you are entitled to some fun and love and someone to share your life with, and ask for their blessing.

Introducing your kids to your partner's kids

Bringing two sets of kids together might be easier than you think: there are more members for the baseball team, and new people to play with rather than their boring old siblings. Sometimes when kids meet other kids they just get on with it, without making too much of a fuss, so long as you adhere to one important condition—they must meet on a level playing field.

> *Keep both sets of kids entirely equal. Same treats, same age-dependent bedtimes, same ground rules.*

The first time you all get together, it's a good idea to head for neutral ground, as kids can get territorial about their own possessions. The older they are, the more you can be open with them and the more you can listen to their opinions about where and how the meeting should take place. Talk to your partner first about what the ground rules of the day will be—where you will eat, how much money will be spent on each child, whether they are allowed candy—and stick to them.

Before the children visit each other's homes, explain the importance of respecting other people's possessions and try to predict possible flash points with your partner before they arise.

- Do you force your kids to eat their greens, while your partner doesn't?
- Is one of you more particular than the other about table manners?
- Do you agree on the number of hours of computer/TV/games console time the kids are allowed per day?
- Do your kids sit down to do their homework as soon as they get in from school or do you let them schedule it themselves?
- How much are your kids required to help around the house? Is it roughly the same as for your partners' kids?
- What about bath times, bedtimes, teeth brushing, and stories?

All these issues and more need to be decided. If you have different styles, introduce changes carefully so that they don't breed resentment when the kids are asked to change their routines.

Explain the reason for any rule changes. If the children are old enough, you could even sit them all around the table to negotiate who does what in the household.

If you are left alone with your partner's children, you need to be able to stop them if they are doing something dangerous—at which stage you will inevitably be told "You're not my mom/dad." But children have an innate sense of fairness and will understand that Josie goes to bed later than they do if she is two years older, but not that she doesn't have to eat spinach while they do.

Negotiating bringing two families together will be a real test of your conflict resolution skills as a couple. Chances are that if you stay together, the kids will be the source of some of your fights in future, even long after they've left home. On page 197 there's advice on how to manage if you all move in together.

WHAT IF YOU DON'T BOND WITH ONE (OR MORE) OF THEIR KIDS?

If you clash with your partner's children, try to figure out the reasons why. It may be that they resent your presence because they would really like their parents to get back together and you stand in the way. It may be that they are getting less one-on-one time with their mom or dad since you came on the scene. Or it could just be a personality clash. It happens. Always remember that you are the grown-up in the situation. Be polite and respectful and stick to the rules of fairness and even-handedness. There may be a breakthrough one day when you come to understand and like each other, or you might just have to count the years until they go off to college.

Dave and Judi

Dave and Judi seemed to have the odds stacked against them. They lived 200 miles apart, they had five children between them—plus she had a cat, while he had a dog and sixteen chickens. They dated for eight weeks before meeting each other's children, by which stage they were sure they wanted to be together. They chose a film followed by a meal to introduce the kids—aged between nine and seventeen. They had discussed it beforehand and were confident the younger kids would be fine, but worried that the teenagers, who could be "moody," might be more of a challenge. There seemed to be an immediate bond, though, and they felt optimistic enough to book a seaside get-away for both families. Once again, it was a huge success, and when Judi's family had to leave a couple of days early, Dave's daughter wrote in her diary: "It won't be the same without them." The family bonding was completed when Judi brought her cat along one day. Despite being a prolific bird-killer at home, it ignored Dave's chickens and made a beeline for the dog, and soon they were rubbing noses with each other and became close. It worked for all concerned, and they've now moved into a big house where they all live together.

Financial matters

In the early stages of a relationship, your partner's finances are really none of your business, as long as they are paying their own way. Without having a specific conversation, you will probably have formed a rough idea of their disposable income from the job they do, the home they live in, the car they drive, and the type of place they tend to suggest eating out in, whether that's a local diner or a swanky five-star restaurant. As things progress, though, and you are considering whether you could have a future together, it's important that you be able to discuss your net worth and your financial priorities. It doesn't need to be approached in a "twenty questions" style, but you should let them know before you get engaged or buy a house together whether you are sinking under the weight of a huge debt—or if you are, in fact, a secret lottery winner.

If you have debts equal to the gross GNP of certain small countries, or have become insolvent in the past, this will affect your credit score and could make it hard for you and your partner to get a mortgage together. You might be nervous about telling them this in the early days, but when you have been together for a few months and your partner has had a chance to see all the positive characteristics you bring to the table, they should be able to take a balanced view.

Similarly, you may be wary of telling someone you have a sizeable inherited fund until you are sure they love you for yourself rather than for your money. It's all about trust. You don't want the other person to feel you are hiding something from them, and you don't want them to hide anything from you.

> *Don't wait too long before divulging your debt mountain or it could seem as though you have been deceitful.*

Think of some conversational openers to help you lead into the subject of money without appearing too nosey:

- What kinds of things make you most stressed?
- Have you ever been really hard up? What's the worst job you've ever had to do?
- What is your dream job? Do you have a plan as to how you'll get it?
- Which of your parents was the saver and which was the spender? (And which one do you take after?)
- What would you do if you won the lottery?

- What do you imagine yourself doing in your retirement?

Follow up whatever they divulge with your own answers, and this should jump-start some kind of honest sharing about your finances. Listen to the underlying assumptions as well as what they are saying and you will learn a lot about their attitudes without asking to scrutinize their bank statements and pay slips.

What if one partner earns much more than the other?

If there is a big divergence in your incomes, it will probably be apparent quite early on, when one partner starts frowning at the price list on a menu or admits they can't afford that skiing weekend in Calgary. If you fall into a situation where the partner who earns the most offers to pay for dinner, vacations, whatever, all of the time, and the partner who earns the least grudgingly agrees, then even with the best will in the world, resentment may still build. Eventually, the high earner may get angry about paying all the time, and the low earner will get angry about being patronized, and things could become critical. Money is one of the most common causes of arguments between married couples. The key, as always, is to talk and agree on how you want to split bills.

In the 21st century, couples come up with all kinds of weird and wonderful ways of dealing with joint finances.

- When you move in together, you can get a joint account into which both salaries go, and out of which all expenses are paid.
- Alternatively, you can keep everything completely separate and when the bills come in, write a check for half each, as roommates might do.
- You can have a joint account into which you each pay the same amount every month, enough to cover joint expenses, then keep the rest of your money in separate accounts to buy things that are just for you.
- Or you could have a joint household account into which each pays according to their income. So, for example, if one partner earns double what the other earns, they pay two-thirds of the household

expenses, while the other pays one-third. Then you both get to keep whatever is left of your salaries for yourself.

There are lots of deals you can strike when you are dating as well.

- If the richer partner wants a pricey meal, they pay for it—but on the understanding that the less-well-off partner will pay the next time you're at a more affordable joint.
- If one partner queues up to get discount theater tickets, the other buys dinner afterwards.
- If you tend to stay at one partner's house most of the time, and they are picking up the household bills (food, electricity, heating), the other partner could treat them to a vacation once a year.

Just be alert for resentments arising if your partner feels they are always paying for your children; or if you turn up in new designer outfits all the time while pleading poverty; or if you buy yourself a luxury car, then say you can't afford to go on a trip together. Make sure both partners feel good about whatever arrangement is reached, and that one partner's ego isn't being dented.

When it comes down to it, your relationship and keeping each other happy is what matters, not how much you earn. If you're a CEO and he's a social worker, you're never going to be on the same salary, so you might as well accept the fact.

THE CHANGING WORKPLACE
More men than women lost their jobs during the 2009 recession, and the types of new jobs being created tend to be in traditionally female areas, so it's increasingly common that women are the primary or, indeed, the only earner in the family. Traditional roles are changing fast and both men and women need to be able to adapt to this.

Special occasions

Among the many compromises you might have to make in a second-time-around relationship is one that can prove to be a bit thorny: Where do you spend vacations and special occasions? First-time-around couples face this dilemma as well, of course, but there are added complications for older couples.

It could be that one or both of you have an elderly parent who, let's face it, might not be around for much longer. You always visit them for certain annual celebrations, and so do your siblings, but your partner wants to be with their children. So do you bring the whole big crowd along and risk the youngsters getting bored in a house that may not have PlayStation and Wii?

What if your kids like to go to your family's cottage by the lake every summer, where they get to go fishing with their cousins and uncles, and everyone mucks in—but your new partner feels like a fish out of water among such a sprawling group of people who've known each other all their lives? Do you go without your partner?

If you both have kids, holiday celebrations may need to be juggled to fit around custody arrangements, and perhaps your partner's kids need to be in San Francisco while yours need to be in San Diego on New Year's Day. Does that mean you and your partner can't be together?

And what if you both have kids from previous marriages and then you have another child of your own? You'll be entering a whole new world of complications and compromises.

The only way to solve these and all the other problems that will arise is to talk and talk and keep talking. Follow the conflict resolution advice on pages 146–152 before your discussion reaches the stage of becoming an actual argument. Make sure each partner is understood, each partner's viewpoints are validated, and each partner feels cared for, as you address every new challenge. There is no one-size-fits-all solution because every family is different, but as long as you keep each other's feelings in mind, you should be able to resolve most things.

Why not bargain with your partner over the trickier issues, almost as you would haggle at a market stall?

- "OK, we'll go to your mom's house for Thanksgiving if we can invite my dad for Christmas."
- "I'll repair your kid's mountain bike if you make a cake for my kid's bake sale."
- "I'm happy to go on vacation with you and your kids but could we get a babysitter and have dinner on our own one or two evenings?"

Once you have made your way through a range of second-time-around minefields, you will be much stronger as a couple. You may even be thinking about making more of a commitment to each other. There's advice on this in the next chapter.

CHAPTER TEN

Preparing for Commitment

How long should you wait for your partner to commit? Here's the magic mathematical formula:

> Take the exact number of weeks you've been together, multiply by the sum of your ages, divide by the number of months your partner's mother nursed them when they were a baby, then subtract the number of times they have uttered the phrase: "Let's just take our time." If the answer is less than 500, you're not quite there yet. If it's over 1,000, you'll never get there. Between 501 and 999—rush down the aisle!

Simple, isn't it? Don't you wish someone had explained that to you before? Unfortunately, it's all nonsense. Like so many rational dilemmas, this one doesn't come with an easy, ready-made answer, because there are way too many variables and two unique personalities to take into account.

Second-time-around couples might get married or choose to live together sooner than first-time-arounders, for many different reasons: they know their own minds better; they've got the money to set up home already, without saving; perhaps they want to have children while there's still time. But while you are weighing whether it is the right decision for you, bear in mind that second-time-around marriages are more likely than first ones to break up. Don't rush into any kind of commitment without thinking through the potential ramifications for you, your family, and your finances. You're not a carefree, penniless student any more, and you could be risking a lot more than a broken heart.

There's no hard and fast rule, but if your friends and family all think you are rushing into a commitment too soon, you should probably heed their warnings.

As a second timer you have a great advantage—your experience. Committing to a long-term relationship the first time can bring a lot of twists and turns because neither partner has had experience in a long-term relationship. But you have, so use that knowledge to plan and prepare for things that younger couples might not know about. Already been a parent? Then you know how much your life will change and how much you have to plan for the event. Bought a house with your ex? Then you know all the pitfalls of making a major purchase together. In this chapter we will make some suggests about how to prepare for commitment—many of which should sound familiar.

DIVORCE RATES

Divorce rates for first-time marriages are currently around 40 percent in the US, down from a peak of 50 percent in the mid 1980s, and these figures are slightly higher in the UK (42.6%) and Australia (46%). However, the divorce rates for second marriages are around 60 percent, and for third ones about 70 percent. There could be all sorts of reasons for this. It might have to do with the additional challenges second-time-around couples face in blending their existing families. It could be because they didn't have as much choice the second time around and settled for less just so they wouldn't be on their own. People who have divorced once already are less likely to have strong religious objections to divorce. And once they've been through it, they know that, while painful, divorce can be a huge relief as well.

What does commitment mean to you?

There are plenty of good reasons for wanting to take the next step in a relationship. For example, a deeper commitment makes sense if you feel that you two have the chance to develop something unbreakable together; if a legal, binding agreement would help to increase the level of trust; if it would make your children feel more secure; or if you feel that you are two soul mates with a high level of compatibility and that you have found the person you want to grow old with.

There are motives that are not as justifiable. A deeper commitment makes less sense if you simply feel you two have been together long enough that your partner is now obligated to commit; or if you are afraid you might never find anyone else; or if you worry that they are less likely to leave if they are wearing the handcuffs of a legal promise.

SIX BAD REASONS FOR GETTING MARRIED

- You think it will make your partner settle down and behave better.
- Your friends and family keep asking when you are going to tie the knot.
- You'll get tax breaks as a married couple.
- You want to make sure your partner doesn't leave you.
- You feel you have to because your partner wants it and you don't like to let them down.
- You're moving in together and could use all the bed linen, towels, and kitchen gadgets you'd get as wedding presents.

There are many ways to increase the commitment between partners, apart from the obvious one of engagement and then marriage.

- Agreeing you are exclusive is a commitment in itself. And once you've both said "I love you," most people accept that the relationship is serious, and that you have certain responsibilities to each other, such as staying faithful, making time to see each other, and considering each other's feelings.

- You could move in together, either as a prelude to marriage at some later date or as an end in itself. This is less common in the US than it is in the UK, where most couples spend a period of time living together before (or instead of) marriage unless they are strongly religious.
- You could buy a house together. This is an important commitment and if you're not married, it's worth having a legal agreement to protect your rights as co-owners and detail what would happen in the event of a relationship breakdown, or if one person was no longer able to meet the repayments.
- You could get a dog together, buy a car together, or start a business together.

All of the above options would give you some kind of increased commitment that would help make the relationship work. Why not start with a slightly lesser commitment as a way of judging what the bigger one will be like? For example, it makes sense to try staying together at least a few days a week before you jointly commit to a crippling mortgage; it makes sense to find out in advance that you absolutely need two bathrooms and that there has to be enough space for all his fishing gear.

Many couples find that caring for a pet together is like a practice run before they have children. If he isn't good at poop scooping, what will he be like when it comes to changing a baby? If she keeps slipping treats to your adorable puppy, you may need to be the disciplinarian when it comes to giving the kids treats.

Of course, these aren't the same types of commitment. Sharing a room a few days a week is a far cry from buying a house together, but the idea is to move into commitment carefully. Every relationship is a learning process, so each step will teach you new lessons about the potential for that relationship.

Why now? There may be practical reasons dictating the timescale: for example, if your lease is about to expire; or if you have a long-distance relationship and are fed up with the commuting; if your biological clock is ticking loudly; or if one of you comes from outside the country and needs to get married in order to be allowed to stay. Perhaps you want to make sure an elderly relative is still around to see you tie the knot. All these are valid reasons for setting a date, but if you don't have any particular time pressure, that will make it easier to agree on a path that you both feel comfortable with. And be sure not to take a step you are not ready for just for practical reasons. It might seem as though living together will make life easier, but not if you end up fighting every day about who does the dishes.

Talking to your partner about commitment

Once you have decided which type of commitment you want, and gathered all the reasons why you want it and why the time is right, then you should sit down and talk to your partner. If you've been together for enough time to know your own minds, the signs are all looking good and you have both declared your love, you should be able to talk about the future without your partner reacting as if you have taken out a gun and threatened them.

Ask your partner where they see the relationship going in the future—and brace yourself for the reply, because it might not be the one you want. If they say they are happy with the way things are, explain your reasons for wanting to move forward to another level of commitment. It may be that they will agree, perhaps with a slightly revised schedule. But if it turns out that they want something different in the future and there's a huge gap between your visions, that doesn't bode well for the success of the relationship.

THE TRUTH ABOUT COMMITMENT PHOBIA

Is your partner emotionally avoidant? Is it fear that is making them shy away from moving in with or marrying you? Have they been burned in the past and are scared of making the same mistake again? Or do they just not love you enough? This is an age-old question that applies to second timers as well as first timers. If you trust that the relationship is moving forward and are happy to wait for a partner to grow into the idea of more commitment, well and good. But if it becomes apparent that they are unwilling to commit to something that you really want, you need to be aware of it. If your partner is reluctant to take the next step, you are entitled to give them an ultimatum: "In or out? Tell me now." Either way, it will make both of your lives better in the long run.

Men are more prone to feeling "trapped" than women. If you are constantly talking about the future and putting pressure on him to get married whenever you are together, there's a good chance that you will scare him—and maybe even scare him away. No one wants to feel as if they have been pressured into a decision, and they will be more committed and happier if they reach that conclusion on their own.

If you are getting lots of enjoyment and fulfillment out of the relationship as it stands, and he is asking you to be patient, the best thing you can do is wait—not necessarily forever, but at least for a while. Enjoy the process and do your best to live in and appreciate the present moment.

Tim and Joy

Tim knew he wanted his proposal to Joy to be special, so he planned it down to the last detail. He told her he was taking her for a surprise day out, beginning with breakfast at her house, which he made. It was a postcard-perfect day, so they took his dog for a long walk around a nearby lake, laughing and talking all the way. In the afternoon, he took her to the art gallery, the place where they'd had their very first date, and they wandered through the exhibits. At three o'clock precisely, Tim made sure they were up on the third floor, where there's a beautiful view. As they stood there, two friends who are professional singers appeared and sang his proposal for him, to the tune of "Daisy, Daisy": "Joyanne, Joyanne, give me your answer do. He's half crazy, all for the love of you." Tim got down on one knee and brought out a ring, but his hand was shaking so much he could hardly slip it on her finger. Joy was giggling with delight, as yet another friend appeared holding a video camera. He had filmed the whole event for them. The onlookers applauded. And, of course, she said yes.

Signs you are with the right person

The person you are with is funny, kind, good-natured, and you love being with them—but are they the right person for you to contemplate spending the rest of your life with? There's no foolproof litmus test, but positive responses to all of the following questions are characteristic of a very special connection between two people who may end up in a successful relationship over the long haul.

Do you share the same life priorities?

Are your long-term career goals compatible? Do you agree on the area where you want to live? Are you happy with the same standard of living, or does one of you want to save up for a bigger house, while the other likes to spend all they earn on luxuries and fine living?

Do you want to have children together? If so, how far would you be prepared to go if it doesn't happen naturally? Would you try IVF, egg donation, surrogacy, or adoption? Or would you just let nature take its course? Do you and your partner have the same views on child rearing? See page 196–197 for more on planning for parenthood.

Are you happy with the way things are right now?

Some couples are always waiting for a mythical future in which their job is no longer stressful, the ex stops being spiteful, the kids calm down and accept their new partner, and they have stopped drinking so much. Both people feel that once the obstacles are removed, they will be truly happy together. Unfortunately, relationships don't work that way. As soon as one problem is resolved, another will pop up and—surprise, surprise!—the couple will still be unhappy.

What people may not realize is that if they are waiting for true happiness, it could mean they are in the wrong relationship. Landing a better job might make life easier financially, but no amount of money will help two people who just aren't good for each other.

The truth is that a happy, well-adjusted couple doesn't have to chase what could be or should be. A good relationship just is.

Do you love each other for who you are?

Is your partner proud of your achievements? Do you ever hear them or her boasting to other people about how great you are? Do they try to change you or are they happy with you just the way you are?

How about you? There are bound to be minor details you would like to fine tune (such as those annoying habits—see page 153) but when you look at your partner for the person they really are, do you feel a rush of love for them?

In good, long-term relationships both partners enjoy the good and accept the not-so-good parts of the other partner. Understanding that you and your partner will not agree on everything and accepting that fact are two very different things, but if you cannot love the other person for who they are, the relationship will most likely founder eventually.

When you love someone, all sorts of minutiae become interesting. Those childhood photo albums and home movies fascinate you for the insights they provide. You might want to know little things, such as what photos they keep on their desk at work, and which salad or sandwich they usually choose for their lunch. You want to know trivia, such as the first album they ever bought, and the first person they kissed in high school. It all builds up the picture of the person who fascinates you more than any other on the planet.

Do you resolve conflict well?

If you replied that you never argue, then you have a problem. Upon closer examination, you'll find that someone in the relationship—perhaps both parties—isn't being forthcoming. Someone's needs and wants aren't being voiced and therefore aren't being addressed.

Having said that, if life is one long drama, where one of you is trying to create high emotions in order to manipulate the other (see page 27), or where there's constant turbulence without some sort of resolution, be careful about committing at this stage.

But what is most important is how you resolve conflict, not the fact that you have conflict; the quality of conflict resolution is a powerful indicator of the quality of the relationship. If you do not engage in a demand-withdraw pattern of interactions, show or feel contempt during conflict, or engage in stonewalling, your relationship stands a much better chance of success.

If you regularly engage in respectful, healthy conflict—without insults or objects being thrown across the room or displays of scorn and contempt—and come out the other side with more understanding of each other, you are onto a good thing. How much a couple fights isn't the issue, unless they don't fight at all.

> *Resolving conflict successfully is one of the key indicators of how well a relationship is working.*

Do most of your friends and family like your partner?

If all the people who love you the most are begging you to get away from someone, then they see some warning signs that you are missing (or not accepting). On the other hand, if the people you trust see what you see in your partner and encourage the relationship, it's a great sign. And if your kids think they are the best thing since Xbox, that's terrific news.

Of course, your friends and family might try to urge you to date someone you would never choose for yourself. In these cases, it's not always wise to follow their advice. But if you're falling in love with someone whom the people in your life are delighted for you to be with, then there's a good chance that this might be the real deal.

Do you know how to make them happy?

If your partner comes in from work buzzing with stress because their boss has just doubled their workload or imposed some unreasonable deadline, do you know how to get them to relax? If they're feeling a bit down, can you cheer them up? If you're male, do you know how to deal with your girlfriend's PMS?

Learning when to make someone laugh and when to offer a sympathetic ear, when to dish up chocolate ice cream, and when a backrub is called for are sensational relationship skills. If you can automatically offer the right thing without even being asked, that is true responsiveness in action that will make your partner feel very loved and valued. Just as important, do they know how to do this for you? These are skills that can be learned, so if your partner is constantly getting better (even if they aren't great at it yet), there is a good chance they will know how to do all of those things soon enough. If that's the case, you've got yourself a "keeper."

Do you both respect each other?

Everyone has their weak spots—maybe they're not so good at wallpapering a room, or their computer skills don't go much further than emailing—but if you want to build a future together, you need to believe that the other person is a competent, talented individual. If you secretly believe they won't ever achieve their long-held dreams of getting a script of theirs made into a feature film, or writing a hit record for Lady Gaga, then it is going to come across in your attitude and introduce a poisonous note, even if nothing is ever said outright. You should be your partner's biggest cheerleader, their most loyal fan.

Mutual respect is crucial for a healthy relationship. Without that respect, there's simply no way to create and build a secure foundation so that you can enjoy all of the benefits of a deep and strong partnership. When you respect your partner and they respect you, the relationship has a good chance of thriving. The communication improves. The commitment deepens. The trust multiplies. You like each other and appreciate the ways you live your individual lives. This is one of the keys to a relationship that will continue to grow and develop over the years.

Matt and Krissie

Matt asked Krissie to marry him in August 2007 after they'd been dating for eleven months. She said yes, and they set the wedding date for June 2008. All was going well until just after New Year, when Matt began to feel unwell. His mind was cloudy, he felt weak, and kept waking up in a sweat. He consulted a doctor, who found a lump in his neck and Hodgkin's lymphoma was diagnosed. He had cancer. He felt he had to give Krissie the chance to walk away if she no longer wanted to marry him, but she said immediately that she wouldn't dream of it. She wanted to be with him—in sickness and in health. At the beginning of March, Matt began sixteen weeks of brutal chemotherapy that made him feel dreadful. So much for your engagement being a happy time! But as rough as the treatment was, he could feel himself slowly improving. He finished chemo eleven days before his wedding and they had a loving, euphoric day—despite his lack of hair! After the honeymoon, they got back home to the best news Matt had had since the day Krissie agreed to marry him: the cancer was in full remission. Matt's health challenge before the wedding day, his bravery in dealing with it, and Krissie's unswerving loyalty and support throughout merely confirmed for them both that they were right for each other.

Planning for Parenthood
(and Step-parenthood)

If neither of you has children from a previous relationship and you're planning to have your first child together, you could be in for a shock. You may think it will bring you closer together, but studies show that couples who have previously always rated their relationship satisfaction right at the top of the scale suddenly experience a dip in contentment after a first child is born. You'll get less sleep, have less money, and spend less time together, so it's completely understandable.

But the more thoroughly you plan for the new arrival, the easier it will be, and the less your relationship will suffer. If you have furnished a nursery, bought plenty of diapers and sterilizing equipment, and arranged for extra help in the house for the first couple of weeks, that's all good. You should also have discussed issues such as how long each partner will take off work, or whether one of you will go back to work at all, and who is going to take on what responsibilities. There are still some people who assume that women will become full-time mothers after childbirth and the man will foot the bill. This is fine if you have both agreed on this arrangement in advance, but not so good if one partner was assuming it would be this way and the other reacts with abject horror.

> *Meticulous planning will help to lessen the shock element of new parenthood, giving you more time to enjoy your baby together.*

If both parents go back to work, what kind of childcare solution will you look for? Don't just expect it to fall into place at the time, because high-quality, affordable childcare is hard to come by. If you don't have a joint account, will you split the cost? And have you discussed what you did and didn't like about your own childhoods and decided roughly how you would like your new family member to be raised?

BECOMING A STEP-PARENT

Step-parenting can be a lonely, thankless task. You're not quite sure what relationship you should have with your partner's children—parent? friend? caterer? taxi driver?—and they don't know what to make of you either. You may find yourself feeling all sorts of dark emotions, such as resentment and jealousy, as your partner prioritizes his kids' happiness over yours—and possibly over that of your children. Fortunately, there are lots of good books offering advice in this area, as well as websites and online forums (see page 216–217). Use them to inspire communication with your partner. Keep talking and resolving conflict calmly and try to ring fence quality time for yourselves, away from all the mayhem.

How about financial plans for the kids' educations, and life insurance in case the main wage earner becomes unable to work for any reason? Have you changed your wills in favor of each other, so that if one person is left behind, they will be able to afford to raise the kids? All these subjects may sound terribly serious and dull when you would much rather sit discussing the baby's name, but financial planning is crucial when you have children. Ultimately, being able to pay for their upbringing will be far more important than a nicely decorated nursery.

All of the same principles apply when you are bringing two families together. If the children are old enough, consult them about whom they will share a bedroom with and what tasks they will be responsible for around the house. Ask them if they foresee any problems ahead and listen to the answers. Make sure each child's voice is heard, and you'll be off to a great start. It's also advisable to make sure that your own children still get quality time alone with you, when they can discuss any worries, no matter how minor, and you can reassure them of your ongoing unconditional love.

Jodie and Joshua

Jodie and Joshua moved in together after dating for two months and they had a year of pure, simple fun, taking trips together, spending most of their time together, and learning about each other. It was going so well that Joshua knew he wanted to marry Jodie and was planning to ask her during the following vacation. But then, tragedy struck when Jodie's sister passed away, leaving behind her three-year-old daughter Serenity. As soon as Joshua heard the news, he knew that he wanted the two of them to adopt the little girl. He proposed to Jodie and they got married soon after, on Valentine's Day; a few months later, the adoption went through. They both knew it would be the end of their carefree lifestyle, but it was a trade-off they soon realized they were happy to make. They love Serenity more than anything and Joshua says that to hear her call him "daddy" is the most wonderful thing he can ever imagine.

Think ahead

None of us can predict what life will throw at us in the future, but one thing's for sure: it will be a mixture of comedy and tragedy. Some plans will work out exactly as we hope and others will have to turn around by 180 degrees in reaction to circumstances. But the more that you plan the transitions—whether combining your finances, or buying a house, or bringing children into your lives—the more you discuss and understand how the process is likely to go, the more you can anticipate where the sore points are likely to be. And then you can deal with them before they go septic.

Lots of couples report that they argue more during their engagement than they ever did before they got engaged, and way more than they do after the wedding. This isn't surprising, because planning a wedding is stressful and this stress can leak into the relationship. On top of this, a couple may be negotiating the structure of the rest of their lives together and coming to realize the magnitude of the step they are taking. This conflict may not be fun, but it offers an opportunity to learn more about each other and what each person needs to pay attention to in the coming years. And at least the issues are being discussed in good time.

If you are standing in the realtor's office, saying, "Gosh, you want a penthouse apartment? I need a house on lots of land," then you've left it rather late.

If you are standing at the altar taking your vows, when she whispers, "You do realize I hate children and don't plan on having any?" this conversation is severely overdue.

These examples are a little over the top, but you get the idea. Before you sign on the dotted line and commit to sharing your life with another person, make sure you've thought through all the predictable stages ahead and discussed them together. The more things you discuss and share with each other, the fewer surprises you will find down the road. That will make the adjustment to being married much easier.

PRE-NUPS

If your partner wants a pre-nuptial agreement, does it mean they are assuming the marriage will fail? It's a tricky subject, fraught with tension, but pre-nups can make sense when there are previous marriages with children to consider. If you are the second wife, coming into the relationship with your own assets, you could find your partner's first wife getting her hands on them if your partner dies or the two of you get divorced. That's not what you'd want, is it? Discuss what you'd like to happen in different eventualities, and if a pre-nup would protect your and your children's assets, it may be the way to go.

CHAPTER ELEVEN

Keeping it Fresh and Fun

If you think a wedding ring on your finger means you can stop working at your relationship, think again. In the US, there's a steady rate of 2 percent of married couples getting divorced each year. In Britain, almost 10 per cent of all divorces are instigated before the second anniversary, implying that some people start feeling taken for granted almost before the confetti has been swept up and the wedding photos admired.

Whether you are married or not, paying attention to certain key aspects of your relationship can keep it growing and deepening over the years. If you keep using them, your relationship skills will continue to improve, so that over the years you will manage conflict more effectively, provide better emotional support for your partner, and celebrate each other's good news as a matter of course.

There are bound to be bad times, when you are not communicating well, but there should also be times when you feel a little pang and realize you are falling more deeply in love.

In this chapter there are some strategies for keeping your relationship strong and healthy. You are probably doing most of them already without thinking about it, but it's worth taking the time to think. Discuss the strategies with your partner and decide how you can adapt them to suit the style of your own unique partnership.

MIND READING

It's a lovely sign of intimacy when you catch your partner's eye and know exactly what they are thinking at that moment. It might be in response to something that has just been said on TV, or when taking the first bite of a dish at a dinner party, and there's a little zing of recognition as you both know you are thinking the same thing. However, beware of expecting your partner to be a mind reader all the time. You're in essence setting them up to fail because no one can succeed all the time, and in fact they will probably fail more often than they'll succeed. Unless you are married to David Blaine or Mysterion the Mindreader, if you want the trash taken out, or the TV turned down because you are on the phone, you'd better just say so.

Novelty is good

Research shows that in the long run, new experiences make people happier than new possessions, and shared experiences are likely to increase satisfaction in a couple. So instead of buying something new, how about trying something new?

Every time you try something new and exciting that neither of you has tried before, you are gaining a special shared experience to add to your collection. It's easy to fall into a routine of work life and home life, a bit of sport at the weekend, and visiting family and friends—which is all fine. But every once in a while, it's good to shake up the mix by adding some new elements. Ever tried gliding? Have you been on an expert-guided walk around your area? Or had a hot-stone massage?

Traveling together is a perfect way to combine lots of new experiences. If you choose somewhere off the beaten tourist track, it will be a real adventure, with lots of joint problem-solving. What's the best way to get from the airport to the place you are staying? Is it safe to eat street food? Where can you change money? How do you get in to that special ceremony in the temple that only happens twice a year? You can both contribute your own skills: one may be better at map-reading, while the other has the gift of the gab. Or if you've gone to a place where neither of you speaks the language, it will be interesting to see who is best at mime!

If you have different tastes in vacations, see if you can combine both approaches. For example, if your partner likes to lie on a beach and tan while you like to visit cultural sites, choose somewhere that combines both, such as Mayan Mexico, or Rio de Janeiro, or Thailand. If one of you likes activity holidays while the other wants the most active thing they do to be turning the pages of a novel, you could split the time so you have active mornings kayaking and lazy afternoons by the pool at your hotel. This way each of you gets to do some of what you like to do, and also try new things out as well.

If you're planning to have kids at a later stage, just think about how the photos and memories of the trips you had together will help build a solid foundation for your relationship. This will help you through all the years of being wakened at 3am, and the tantrums of the terrible twos. Even a week's trip can fill a whole new photo album of shared experiences and joint memories that you'll be able to cherish forever.

Have a joint project

For many couples, their joint project will be doing up their home. In this day and age, home improvement is a massive growth industry, whether you are knocking down walls and building extensions, or simply giving the kitchen a new color scheme. If you both get involved, contributing whatever skills you have and learning new ones along the way, the result should be a win-win situation: you become closer as a couple and you also get to live in a nicer home. (This is drawing a veil over potential disasters when one of you leans against a freshly painted wall and the other gets the measurements wrong so the new kitchen units don't fit.)

Of course, raising children together is a "project" in itself. Some people think that having children will act as relationship glue, but the opposite can often be the case. Children can put intolerable strain on a relationship that is not already in good shape, and can rock even a solid couple from time to time. You need to have a life as a couple outside your roles as parents to help you stand shoulder to shoulder during the inevitable kid-related crisis points.

If you are both creative, perhaps you could write a book together, or make a movie, or record an album. If you are more practical, you could buy an old boat and do it up, or create a vegetable garden, or build a log cabin in the woods.

As the years go by, you are likely to develop more shared interests, because that's what happens with long-term couples anyway, but creating something together that you are both proud of can be a lovely way to cement your relationship.

Damien and Pauline

Pauline and Damien arranged to meet in a park for their first date, and she was surprised and delighted when he produced a small picnic of salmon, cheese, and chocolate, complete with a wine cooler and even mosquito repellent. She couldn't stop smiling at the effort he had gone to. During the date they realized that they only lived six minutes from one another and they began to see each other daily.

Six months on they took a vacation together, and one morning Damien suggested they go for a walk on the beach. They reached a rock pool and Pauline spotted a clear glass bottle with a message inside. She opened the message to find it was addressed to her from Damien and it was asking her to marry him. She had no hesitation in accepting.

Those who play together, stay together

Sharing leisure activities is a strong indicator of a successful relationship. This could mean playing golf together, or playing tennis, or playing cards—whatever floats your boat. But it is also important to be play-*ful*. It's good to tap into your inner kid—flicking water at each other as you clear the dinner table, or throwing a handful of grass as you mow the lawn. Private jokes that no one else understands are a great form of intimacy, especially when no one else has a clue why you both crack up at the mention of "pickled herrings" or "Yogi Bear."

> *If you're good at making your partner laugh you are probably in for a long and successful marriage.*

Have you ever stopped in mid-argument, looked at each other, and suddenly burst into fits of laughter? The couples who are best at resolving conflict are able to introduce some kind of positive emotion in the heat of the moment. Other couples might just gather furious momentum like a runaway train getting faster and faster as it heads for the buffers, with nothing to put the brakes on the negative emotions. But if you can introduce something to break the tension and even induce a titter, it will help to produce a change in the physiological stress response to the argument. You might go straight back to arguing, and even get heated again, but then something else makes you laugh and the whole negative process of the fight is turned around.

When the bills are piling up, the kids are fighting, the house is a mess, and you're feeling stressed, it's easy to start getting weighed down by it all. Sure, you should support your partner when times are rough, and they should support you—but don't forget to have fun along the way. Tease each other when you need to lighten the atmosphere. Being part of a couple is not some duty you have to fulfill; it should be mutually enjoyable as well.

DON'T BE A MARTYR

If you are unhappy about the division of labor in the household, don't let it fester. Sit down with a notepad and pen and renegotiate the terms of engagement. Write a long list of everything that has to be done and how frequently, then take turns to choose which chores you want to be responsible for. If there are jobs you both hate—or enjoy—you can alternate, but don't make it so complicated you need a computer program to figure out whose turn it is to clean the oven.

Smooching and snuggling

Studies show that plenty of non-sexual affectionate touching is a great predictor of relationship success. Being overtly affectionate with each other on a daily basis is more important than having sex once a week. Ruffling her hair as she cooks the dinner, rubbing his shoulders as he sits at the computer, cuddling up as you watch TV, walking arm in arm, or just a light touch of the leg in passing are all reminders that you love each other. When your partner caresses you and you reciprocate, it's a form of appropriate responsiveness, a little signal of your togetherness. Choose your own style. Some people think it's soppy to hold hands, while others don't like being affectionate in public—doesn't matter what you do so long as it's regular and loving.

Being affectionate to each other on a daily basis would be more important for the relationship than having sex once a week.

Sexual touching is great as well but make sure it's not always about foreplay but sometimes just play. A sexual touch becomes loaded if it comes with the expectation of intercourse at a time when you may not feel like it. But if it's just for the fun of it, because you fancy each other and no one else is watching, then why not?

If you feel your sex life has got into a rut, there are loads of books and websites with advice for sparking it up again. But married couples tend to like their own comfortable routine of married sex better than any number of one-night flings. When you are making love for the hundredth or thousandth time, you know exactly which positions are best for both of you and how to make each other happy. You will have advanced bedroom skills tailored to meet each other's needs and you choose to have sex as an expression of love (as well as sexiness.)

The eHarmony Longitudinal Study of Marriage

In 2008, 300 married couples volunteered to take part in a five-year-long study to find out what makes marriage successful. Each person answered questionnaires about their family background, personality and emotional temperament, their relationship history, and their own views on the quality of their marriage. They were questioned separately about issues such as how responsive their partner is, how good he or she is at comforting them, and how well they resolve conflict.

As well as listening to their own views, researchers invited them to sit in a closed room and have a number of interactions, which were filmed and examined. They teased each other, talked about a positive event that had happened to them personally, tried to resolve a conflict, and helped their partner deal with something they wanted to change about themselves. As well as listening to what the couples actually said, researchers looked at how they said it, the amount of eye contact they had with each other, and their body language throughout, in order to analyze how well their relationship was going.

The goal of the study is to increase our understanding of what makes a marriage successful, and pinpoint ways in which couples can keep their relationships strong over the years. One thing that has become clear already is that the time these couples are spending thinking about their relationships is having beneficial effects.

Under normal circumstances, men tend to feel stressed and threatened if their partners announce that they want to sit down and have a discussion about the state of the relationship. They think: "Uh-oh. I've done something wrong and am going to get told off." Either that or they might assume you will be fishing for more commitment: "Where is this relationship going? How do you see the future?" In both cases, they are likely to try and withdraw. Women, on the other hand, like to analyze their relationships and talk through problems, even before they arise. You need to find ways of engaging your partner without them feeling threatened, and one way of doing this might be to take the following quiz, partly based on the eHarmony Longitudinal Study, to assess the health of your own relationship. Keep it light and fun rather than setting it up as a big challenge on which a lot rides, but take note of any issues that arise.

Test your own relationship

The following questions are based on the work of three different groups of eminent researchers in the field of relationships. If you want to find more about their work, you'll find full citations in the Notes on page 221. To complete the quiz, simply make a couple of photocopies of it, circle your answers, and total your score, then get your partner to do the same.

The first set of questions is based on the Couples Satisfaction Index, which was created by Janette Funk and Ron Rogge at the University of Rochester. The higher your score, the more satisfied you are with your relationship—that is, the more you find the relationship rewarding, happy, and comfortable.

Q: **How happy are you in your relationship?**

A: 1 Extremely unhappy 2 Fairly unhappy 3 A little unhappy
4 Happy 5 Very happy 6 Extremely happy 7 It's perfect

Q: **My relationship is warm and comfortable. Is this statement:**

A: 1 Never true 2 Rarely true 3 Somewhat true 4 Mostly true
5 Almost completely true 6 Completely true?

Q: **How rewarding is your relationship?**

A: 1 Not rewarding at all 2 A little rewarding 3 Somewhat
rewarding 4 Mostly rewarding 5 Almost completely rewarding
6 Completely rewarding

Q: **How satisfied are you with your relationship?**

A: 1 Not satisfied at all 2 A little satisfied 3 Somewhat satisfied
4 Mostly satisfied 5 Almost completely satisfied 6 Completely
satisfied

The next set of questions is based on the Intimacy Process Model
created by Harry Reis at Rochester University and Phil Shaver at
the University of California, Davis. The higher you score, the more
intimacy you perceive in your relationship—that is, the more you think
your partner understands, cares for, and validates you.

Q: **How well does your partner understand you?**

A: 1 Doesn't understand me at all 2 Understands me a little
3 Somewhat understands me 4 Understands me 5 Understands
me well 6 Understands me very well 7 Understands me
completely

Q: **How much does your partner care about you?**

A: 1 Doesn't care about me at all 2 Cares about me very little
3 Cares about me a little 4 Somewhat cares about me 5 Cares
about me 6 Cares about me a lot 7 Cares about me completely

Q: **How much does your partner validate you by confirming or endorsing you and your beliefs?**

A: 1 Doesn't validate me at all 2 Validates me very little 3 Validates me a little 4 Somewhat validates me 5 Validates me 6 Validates me a lot 7 Validates me completely

The final questions are based on the Investment Model Scale, which measures how committed you are to the relationship. The higher you score, the more you are committed to your relationship and think that the alternatives to your relationship are not attractive.

Q: **I am committed to continuing this relationship. Do you:**

A: 1 Disagree completely 2 Disagree a lot 3 Disagree a little
4 Neither disagree or agree 5 Agree a little 6 Agree a lot
7 Agree completely?

Q: **There are plenty of other people out there to date if this relationship doesn't work out. Do you:**

A: 7 Disagree completely 6 Disagree a lot 5 Disagree a little
4 Neither disagree or agree 3 Agree a little 2 Agree a lot
1 Agree completely?

Q: **I have invested a lot in this relationship. Do you:**

A: 1 Disagree completely 2 Disagree a lot 3 Disagree a little
4 Neither disagree or agree 5 Agree a little 6 Agree a lot
7 Agree completely?

Satisfaction, intimacy, and commitment are three critical components in a relationship. The stronger each of these components, the more likely you are to have a successful relationship that is satisfying and rewarding to both you and your partner.

If you've done the math, you'll realize that the top score possible is 60. Most couples score very high on all of these scales in the passionate early stages of a relationship, but over time this will change, going down, and sometimes back up again.

One of the most important things in understanding these measures is not the absolute score out of 60, but the way in which your relationship changes over time. If you (or your partner) experience a sudden sharp dip in one of these scales you should be wary because you may be going through a rough patch. If you find that your score steadily decreases over time it might be a signal that you need to reinvigorate your relationship, or it could just reflect stressful life circumstances. For example, if you have recently had a child, your satisfaction with the relationship can decrease because you have less sleep, less money, and less time for each other.

It could be very helpful for you and your partner to take this quiz about your relationship every three or six months, almost like a little check-up to make sure things are going well. Use it as a standard to check in on your relationship every once in a while to make sure it is still healthy and strong.

Being attentive

If you've gotten this far in a book about relationships, it means you are serious about getting your own partnership to work—and that's a great sign. Look around at all your friends who are single and can't find the right person, or those who are unhappy in their relationships but sticking together "for the sake of the kids" or because they "can't afford to break up." Now pat yourself on the back. You already know that it's not luck that makes a relationship work long term; it's not astrology, or fate, or your reward for leading a good life in your previous incarnation. It's down to the intelligence and attention you apply now, in the present, to considering another person's feelings as well as your own.

Checking in and taking the temperature of the relationship every few months could make a big difference to its success.

It takes quite a lot of effort to build and maintain a successful relationship, but the rewards are huge and ongoing so it's an investment well worth making. You get someone to bounce ideas off, someone to cuddle up to, someone to make you laugh, someone to take care of you when you're sick and celebrate with when times are good. Hopefully you will have a great relationship for the rest of your life. And statistically, you are likely to live longer if you're in a good relationship than you would if you were single.

If you haven't already found that person, why not get out there and make a start? The sooner you find them, the longer you'll have together. If you think you've got the right partner already, use the advice in this book to nurture your relationship and keep it strong in the years to come. And go and give them a big hug right now!

ABOUT eHARMONY

eHarmony (www.eharmony.com) was founded in 2000 and pioneered the use of relationship science to match singles seeking long-term relationships. Today, the company offers a variety of relationship services in the United States, Canada, Australia, the United Kingdom, and Brazil—with members in more than 150 countries around the world. According to a 2009 study Harris Interactive conducted for eHarmony, an average of 542 people per day get married in the United States after meeting through the online matchmaker.

Following a 35-year career as a clinical psychologist, eHarmony founder Dr. Neil Clark Warren decided there had to be a better way for people to find love than leaving it entirely to chance. He observed that in many cases, marriages successfully stood the test of time when both partners were fundamentally compatible. With this initial insight, Dr. Warren and eHarmony's founding research team set out to scientifically test the theory that compatibility leads to a greater likelihood of long-term relationship satisfaction. They also set out to identify the qualities that best predict long-term relationship success.

After evaluating thousands of married couples in the United States on their marital satisfaction, they determined the distinguishing traits and qualities that the happiest couples shared.

Based on these insights, they developed a series of statistical models to predict, with a high degree of confidence, which pairings of single individuals could mirror the qualities that the most-satisfied married couples shared. This process identified the 29 Dimensions® of Compatibility—the shared values, beliefs, attitudes, and personality traits—that are powerful predictors of marital satisfaction. These compatibility qualities became the backbone of eHarmony's online match-making service.

eHarmony is the only online dating site that continues to invest in its relationship science by operating an observational research laboratory at its California headquarters. This research contributes to the international academic community's understanding of how relationships form and change over time. It also ensures the company's matching models remain current and responsive to users' needs.

Singles who use the eHarmony service begin by completing a comprehensive Relationship Questionnaire. The results are analyzed and potential matches are suggested, based on the 29 Dimensions of Compatibility. Members can then refine their selection criteria and identify some of their hobbies and interests to expand or narrow their pool of potential mates.

eHarmony also offers a structured and secure way for people to correspond with each other. Known as Guided Communication, the four-step process helps singles find out important information about their matches early on, without having to divulge personal contact details until they are comfortable doing so.

eHarmony also operates a free eHarmony Advice site with insightful dating and relationship articles, and community-led discussion boards.

Millions of people around the world have used eHarmony to find their ideal match, and the success stories speak for themselves. To read some of them, visit eHarmony's fan page on Facebook: **www.facebook.com/eharmony**.

To find out more about eHarmony, or to sign up, visit the website at: **www.eharmony.com**

Or, in the UK: **www.eharmony.co.uk**

Or, in Australia: **www.eharmony.com.au**

DR. GIAN GONZAGA, PH.D.

Dr. Gonzaga is the senior director of research and development at eHarmony. He is also the head of eHarmony Labs, the California-based research center set up to study what makes relationships successful. He has taught, presented, and published extensively on topics relating to relationships, love, and health. He has received numerous honors and awards for his work, including the prestigious National Science Foundation minority Predoctoral Fellowship and Psi Chi National Undergraduate Research Competition.

He is a member of several professional and academic associations, including the American Psychological Association, the American Psychological Society, the Society for Personality and Social Psychology, and the International Society for the Study of Personal Relationships.

Dr. Gonzaga holds a doctorate in Personality-Social Psychology from the University of California, Berkeley, and a bachelor's degree in psychology from Gettysburg College in Gettysburg, Pennsylvania.

USEFUL WEBSITES

Note that eHarmony has no commercial links to any of the organizations featured and does not necessarily endorse any of these sites or organizations. This list is a reference guide only.

USA

Counseling and therapy
American Counseling Association
www.counseling.org/

The Family & Marriage Counseling Directory
www.family-marriage-counseling.com

MarriageAdvice.com
www.marriageadvice.com

American Assocation for Marriage & Family Therapy
www.aamft.org/

American Psychological Association
www.apa.org

International Association for Marriage and Family Counseling
www.iamfc.org

Marriage Success Training
www.stayhitched.com

Support for domestic violence
The National Domestic Violence Hotline
www.thehotline.org and

National Network to End Domestic Violence
www.nnedv.org
24-hour Helpline: 1 800 799 SAFE (7233)

National Coalition Against Domestic Violence
www.ncadv.org

Single parenting
Parents Without Partners
www.parentswithoutpartners.org

National Association of Single Mothers
www.singlemothers.org
Center for SPFM: Single Parent Family Ministry
www.spfm.com

Single Mom
www.singlemom.com

Support following bereavement
Grief Counselor
www.griefcounselor.org

Grief Net
www.griefnet.org

Step-parenting and blended families
National Stepfamily Resource Center
www.stepfamilies.info

StepTalk.org
www.steptalk.org

Step Family Tips
www.stepfamilytips.com

I Do! Take Two
www.idotaketwo.com

Second Wives Club
www.secondwivesclub.com

Blending a Family
www.blendingafamily.com

UK

Counselling and therapy
The British Association for Counselling and Psychotherapy
www.bacp.co.uk

British Association for Sexual and Relationship Therapy
www.basrt.org.uk

International Stress Management Association (ISMA)
www.isma.org.uk

National Association for Mental Health (MIND)
www.mind.org.uk

Relate
www.relate.org.uk

British Association for Behavioural and Cognitive Psychotherapies
www.babcp.com
One Plus One Marriage and Partnership Research
www.oneplusone.org.uk

Marriage Care
www.marriagecare.org.uk

Support for domestic violence
Victim support
www.victimsupport.org

Respect
www.respect.uk.net

Women's Aid National Domestic Violence
www.womensaid.org.uk

Domestic Violence 24-hour Helpline:
08457 023 468

Men Experiencing Domestic Abuse (MEDA)
24-hour Helpline: 01686 629114

Single parenting
Lone Parents
www.lone-parents.org.uk

Gingerbread
www.gingerbread.org.uk

One Space
www.onespace.org.uk

Support following bereavement
Cruse Bereavement Care
www.crusebereavementcare.org.uk

Bereavement UK
www.bereavementuk.co.uk

Step-parenting and blended families
Being a Stepparent
www.beingastepparent.co.uk

Parentline Plus
www.parentlineplus.org.uk

The Institute of Family Therapy
www.instituteoffamilytherapy.org.uk

Care for the Family
www.careforthefamily.org.uk

The British Second Wives Club
www.thebritishsecondwivesclub.co.uk

The Parent Connection
www.theparentconnection.org.uk

The Centre for Separated Families
www.separatedfamilies.info

Australia

Counselling and therapy
Australian Association of Relationship
Counsellors
www.aarc.org.au
Relationships Australia
www.relationships.com.au

Relationship Help Online
www.relationshiphelponline.com.au

Australian Counselling Association
www.theaca.net.au

The Psychotherapy and Counselling
Federation of Australia
www.pacfa.org.au

Sexual Health Australia (SHA)
www.sexualhealthaustralia.com.au

Support for domestic violence
Life Line Australia
www.lifeline.org.au

Domestic Violence & Incest Resource
Centre
www.dvirc.org.au

Dads in Distress
www.dadsindistress.asn.au

Men's Line Australia
www.menslineaus.org.au
24-hour Helpline: 1300 78 99 78

Single parenting
Raising Children Network
www.raisingchildren.net.au

National Council for Single Mothers and
Their Children
www.ncsmc.org.au

Parents Without Partners Australia
www.pwpaustralia.net

Support following bereavement
Australian Centre for Grief and
Bereavement
www.grief.org.au

The Bereavement Care Centre
www.bereavementcare.com.au

Step-parenting and blended families
Stepfamilies Australia
www.stepfamily.org.au

Family Relationships Online
www.familyrelationships.gov.au

StepfamilyZone
www.stepfamily.asn.au

Parenting Research Centre
www.parentingrc.org.au

NOTES

Chapter 1

Terracciano, A., McCrae, R. R., & Costa, P. T. (2010). "Intra-individual change in personality stability and age." *Journal of Research in Personality*, 44, 31-37.

Dweck, C. S., & Ehrlinger, J. (2006). "Implicit theories and conflict resolution." In. Deutsch, M.; Coleman, P. T.; Marcus, E. C. (Eds.) (2006). *The handbook of conflict resolution: Theory and practice* (2nd Ed), (pp. 317-330). Hoboken, NJ, US: Wiley Publishing.

Rotter, J.B. (1954). *Social Learning and Clinical Psychology*. New York: Prentice-Hall.

Miller, P. C., Lefcourt, H. M., & Ware, E. E. (1983). "The construction and development of the Miller Marital Locus of Control scale." *Canadian Journal of Behavioural Science*, 15, 266-279.

Story, L. B., & Repetti, R. (2006). "Daily occupational stressors and marital behaviour." *Journal of Family Psychology*, 20, 690-700.

Chapter 2

Hazan, C., & Shaver, P. (1987). "Romantic love conceptualized as an attachment process." *Journal of Personality and Social Psychology*, 52, 511-524.

Shaver, P., Hazan, C., & Bradshaw, D. (1988). "Love as attachment: The integration of three behavioral systems." In R. J. Sternberg & M. L. Barnes (Eds.), *The Psychology of Love* (pp. 68-99). New Haven, CT: Yale University Press.

Downey, G., Freitas, A. L., Michealis, B., & Khouri, H. (1998). "The self-fulfilling prophecy in close relationships: Do rejection sensitive women get rejected by romantic partners?" *Journal of Personality and Social Psychology*, 75, 545-560.

Gottman, J. (1994). *Why Marriages Succeed or Fail...and How You Can Make Yours Last*. Simon & Schuster.

Gottman, J. (1994). *The Seven Principles for Making Marriage Work*. Crown Publishers.

Pennebaker, J.W. (2004). *Writing to heal: A guided journal for recovering from trauma and emotional upheaval*. Oakland, CA: New Harbinger Press.

Pennebaker, J.W. (1991). "Self-expressive writing: Implications for health, education, and welfare". In S.I. Fontaine, P. Elbow, & P. Belanoff (Eds.), *Nothing begins with N: New investigations of freewriting* (pp. 157-172). Carbondale, IL: Southern Illinois Press.

Depaulo, B. M. & Morris, W. L., (2005). "Singles in society and in science." *Psychological Inquiry*, 16, 57-83.

Chapter 3

Acitelli, L. K., Kenny, D. A., & Weiner, D. (2001). "The importance of similarity and understanding of partners' marital ideals to relationship satisfaction." *Personal Relationships*, 8, 167-185.

Anderson, C., Keltner, D., & John, O. P. (2003). "Emotional convergence between people over time." *Journal of Personality and Social Psychology*, 84, 1054-1068.

Berscheid, E., Dion, K., Hatfield, E., & Walster, G. W. (1971). "Physical attractiveness and dating choice: A test of the matching hypothesis." *Journal of Experimental Social Psychology*, 7, 173-189.

Byrne, D. (1971). *The Attraction Paradigm*. New York: Academic Press.

Condon, J. W., & Crano, W. D. (1988). "Implied evaluation and the relationship between similarity and interpersonal attraction." *Journal of Personality and Social Psychology*, 54, 789-797.

Dryer, D. C, & Horowitz, L. M. (1997). "When do opposites attract? Interpersonal Complementarity versus similarity." *Journal of Personality and Social Psychology*, 72, 592-603.

Gonzaga, G. C., Campos, B., & Bradbury, T. (in press). "Similarity, convergence, and relationship satisfaction in dating and married couples." *Journal of Personality and Social Psychology*.

Kiesler, S. B., & Baral, R. L. (1970). "The search for the romantic partner: The effects of self-esteem and physical attractiveness on romantic behavior." In K. Gergen & D. Marlow (Eds.), *Personality and Social Behavior*. Reading, MA: Addison-Wesley.

Luo, S., & Klohnen, E. C. (2005). "Assortative mating and marital quality in newlyweds: A couple-centered approach." *Journal of Personality and Social Psychology*, 88, 304-326.

Rosenbaum, M. E. (1986). "The repulsion hypothesis: On the nondevelopment of relationships." *Journal of Personality and Social Psychology*, 51, 1156-1166.

Watson, D., Klohnen, E. C., Casillas, A., Nus Simms, E., & Haig, J. (2004). "Match makers and deal breakers: Analyses of assortative mating in newlywed couples," *Journal of Personality and Social Psychology*, 72, 1029-1068.

Buss, D. M. & Barnes, M. (1986). "Preferences in human mate selection," *Journal of Personality and Social Psychology*, 50, 559-570.

Garver-Apgar, C. E., Gangestad, S. W., Thornhill, S. W., Miller, R. D., & Olp, J. J. (2006). "Major Histocompatibility Complex alleles, sexual responsivity, and unfaithfulness in romantic couples," *Psychological Science*, 17, 830-835.

Gable, S. L., Gonzaga, G. C., & Strachman, A. (2006). "Will you be there for me when things go right? Social support for positive events." *Journal of Personality and Social Psychology*, 91, 904-917.

Bolger, N., Zuckerman, A., Kessler, R. C. (2000). "Invisible Support and adjustment to stress." *Journal of Personality and Social Psychology*, 79, 953-961.

Bolger, N., & Amarel, D. (2007)."Effects of social support visibility on adjustment to stress: Experimental evidence." *Journal of Personality and Social Psychology*, 92, 458-475.

Henderson, L. & Zimbardo, P. G. (2001). "Shyness as a clinical condition: The Stanford model." In Crozier, W. Ray (Ed) & Alden, Lynn E. (Ed), (2001). *International handbook of social anxiety: Concepts, research and interventions relating to the self and shyness*, (pp. 431-447). New York, NY, US: John Wiley & Sons Ltd.

DeKoning, E., & Weiss, R. L. (2002). "The relational humor inventory: Functions of humor in close relationships." *The American Journal of Family Therapy*, 30, 1-18.

Ziv, A., & Gadish, O. (1988). "Humor and marital satisfaction." *The Journal of Social Psychology*, 129, 759-768.

Chapter Six

Gonzaga, G. C., Keltner, D., Londahl, E. A., & Smith, M. D. (2001). "Love and the commitment problem in romantic relations and friendship." *Journal of Personality and Social Psychology*, 81, 247-262

Gonzaga, G. C., Turner, R. A., Keltner, D., Campos, B. C., & Altemus, M. (2006). "Romantic love and sexual desire in close bonds." *Emotion*, 6, 163-179.

Grammer, K. (1990). "Strangers meet: Laughter and nonverbal signs of interest in opposite-sex encounters." *Journal of Nonverbal Behavior*, 14, 209-236.

Moore, M. M. (1985). "Nonverbal courtship patterns in women: Context and consequences." *Ethology and Sociobiology*, 6, 237-247.

Chapter Seven

Gable, S. L., Reis, H. T., Impett, E. A., & Asher, E. R. (2004). "What do you do when things go right? The intrapersonal and interpersonal benefits of sharing positive events." *Journal of Personality and Social Psychology*, 87, 228-245.

Reis, H. T., Clark, M. S., & Holmes, J. G. (2004). "Perceived partner responsiveness as an organizing construct in the study of intimacy and closeness". In Mashek, D. J. & Aron, A. P. (Eds.), (2004). *Handbook of Closeness and Intimacy*, (pp. 201-225). Mahwah, NJ, US: Lawrence Erlbaum Associates Publishers.

Chapter Eight

Impett, E., Strachman, A., Finkel, E., & Gable., S. (in press). "Maintaining sexual desire and sexual satisfaction: The importance of approach relationship goals." *Journal of Personality and Social Psychology*.

Algoe, S.B., Fredrickson, B.L., Gable, S.L., & Strachman, A. "Beyond 'Thanks!' Expressions of appreciation as relationship glue." Presentation given at the Society for Personality and Social Psychology Conference, Las Vegas, NV January 2010.

Algoe, S., Gable, S., & Maisel, N. (2010). "It's the little things: Everyday gratitude as a booster shot for romantic relationships." *Personal Relationships*, 17 (2), 217-233.

Woznicki, K. "A little gratitude keeps relationships strong." Web MD, May 24, 2010.

Dutton, D. G., & Aron, A. P. (1974). "Some evidence for heightened sexual attraction under conditions of high anxiety." *Journal of Personality and Social Psychology*.

Reis, H. T., Clark, M. S., & Holmes, J. G. (2004). "Perceived Partner Responsiveness as an Organizing Construct in the Study of Intimacy and Closeness." In. Mashek, D. J. (Ed); Aron, A. P. (Ed), (2004). *Handbook of Closeness and Intimacy*, (pp. 201-225). Mahwah, NJ, US: Lawrence Erlbaum Associates Publishers.

Gable, S. L., Gonzaga, G. C., & Strachman, A. (2006). "Will you be there for me when things go right? Social support for positive events." *Journal of Personality and Social Psychology*, 91, 904-917.

Verhoftstadt, L. L., Buysse, A., Ickes, W., Davis, M., & Devoldre, I. (2008). "Support provision in marriage: The role of emotional similarity and empathic accuracy." *Emotion*, 8, 792-802.

Bolger, N., Zuckerman, A., & Kessler, R. C. (2000). "Invisible Support and adjustment to stress." *Journal of Personality and Social Psychology*, 79, 953-961.

Sullivan, K. T., Pasch, L. A., Johnson, M. D., & Bradbury, T. N. (2010). "Social support, problem solving, and the longitudinal course of newlywed marriage." *Journal of Personality and Social Psychology*, 98, 631-644.

Gottman, J. (1994). *Why Marriages Succeed or Fail...and How You Can Make Yours Last*. Simon & Schuster.

Gottman, J. (1994). *The Seven Principles for Making Marriage Work*. Crown Publishers.

Heavey, C. L., Christensen, A., & Malamuth, N. M. (1995). "The longitudinal impact of demand and withdrawal during marital conflict." *Journal of Consulting and Clinical Psychology*, 63, 797-801.

Reis, H. T., & Shaver, P. (1988). "Intimacy as an interpersonal process." In Duck, Steve; Hay, Dale F.; Hobfoll, Stevan E. ; Ickes, William & Montgomery, Barbara M. (Eds.), (1988). *Handbook of personal relationships: Theory, research and interventions* (pp. 367-389). Oxford, England: John Wiley & Sons.

Fincham, F., & Beach, S. R. H. (2007). "Forgiveness and martial quality: Precursor or consequence in well-established relationships?" *Journal of Positive Psychology*, 2, 260-268.

Cunningham, M. R., Barbee, A. P., & Druen, P. B. (1997). "Social allergens and the reactions they produce: Escalation of annoyance and disgust in love and work." In R. M. Kowalski (Ed.) *Aversive Personal Behaviors*, (pp. 189-214). New York, NY, USA: Plenum Press.

Chapter Nine

Allen, E. S., Atkins, D. C., Baucom, D. H., Snyder, D. K., Gordon, K. C., & Glass, S. P. (2005). "Intrapersonal, interpersonal, and contextual factors in engaging in and responding to extramarital involvement." *Clinical Psychology: Science and Practice*, 12, 100-130.

Chapter Eleven

Verhoftstadt, L. L., Buysse, A., Ickes, W., Davis, M., & Devoldre, I. (2008). "Support provision in marriage: The role of emotional similarity and empathic accuracy." *Emotion*, 8, 792-802.

Dutton, D. G., & Aron, A. P. (1974). "Some evidence for heightened sexual attraction under conditions of high anxiety." *Journal of Personality and Social Psychology*.

DeKoning, E., & Weiss, R. L. (2002). "The relational humor inventory: Functions of humor in close relationships." *The American Journal of Family Therapy*, 30, 1-18.

Ziv, A., & Gadish, O. (1988). "Humor and marital satisfaction." *The Journal of Social Psychology*, 129, 759-768.

Emmons, R. A., & McCullough, M. E. (2003). "Counting blessings versus burdens: An experimental investigation of gratitude and subjective well being in daily life." *Journal of Personality and Social Psychology*, 84, 377-389.

Reis, H. T., & Shaver, P. (1988). "Intimacy as an interpersonal process." In Duck, S., Hay, D. F., Stevan E., Ickes, W., & Barbara, M, (Eds), *Handbook of Personal Relationships: Theory, Research, and Interventions*, (pp. 367-389). Oxford, England: John Wiley and Sons.

Funk, J. L., & Rogge, R. D., (2007). "Testing the ruler with item response theory: Increasing the precision of measurement for relationship satisfaction with the couples satisfaction index." *Journal of Family Psychology*, 21, 572-583.

Rusbult, C. E., Martz, J. M., & Agnew, C. R. (1998). "The investment model scale: Measuring commitment level, satisfaction level, quality of alternatives, and investment size." *Personal Relationships*, 5, 357-391.

ACKNOWLEDGMENTS

Dr. Gonzaga would like to thank everyone on the eHarmony team for the work they have done to make this book possible. Specifically, thanks to Dr. Galen Buckwalter, Dr. Steven Carter, Dr. Erina Lee, Dr. Amy Strachman, and Heather Setrakian for the research they have conducted for eHarmony and eHarmony Labs. Thanks to Kolby Kirk, Erica Scheer, and Emily Mayfield for their endless support in the research department. Thanks to Grant Langston, Jeannie Assimos, Amanda Paxson, Tony Horkins, Keith Wall, and Julia Filsell for the wonderful advice they have given for both singles and people in relationships. Thanks to Greg Waldorf, Cary Berger and Steve Nikkhou for all of their advice. And most importantly, thanks to Helen Melluish for making this project happen.

Grateful thanks to all of the relationship scientists and academics who have worked for many years to discover the secrets of what makes relationships successful and satisfying. Without their tireless efforts none of this book would be possible.

Thanks to Stephanie Jackson and Denise Bates from Octopus Publishing in London, and to Gill Paul for assisting in the creation and editing of this book.

Finally, special thanks to Dr. Neil Clark Warren. His founding research and vision to create more love in the world has enabled eHarmony to successfully match millions of people in over 150 countries.

INDEX